Derek S. Hopson, Ph.D.,
and Darlene Powell Hopson, Ph.D.

▲▽▲▽▲▽▲▽▲▽▲▽▲▽▲▽▲

FRIENDS,

LOVERS,

▲▽▲▽▲▽ # AND

a guide

to better

relationships # SOUL

between

black men

and women # MATES

▲▽▲▽▲▽▲▽▲▽▲▽▲▽▲▽▲

SIMON & SCHUSTER
New York London Toronto Sydney Tokyo Singapore

SIMON & SCHUSTER
Rockefeller Center
1230 Avenue of the Americas
New York, New York 10020

Designed by Songhee Kim
Manufactureed in the United States of America

10 9 8 7 6 5 4 3 2 1

Library of Congress Cataloging-in-Publication Data
Hopson, Derek S.
    Friends, lovers, and soul mates : a guide to better relation-
ships between Black men and women / Derek S. Hopson and
Darlene Powell Hopson.
        p.   cm.
    Includes bibliographical references (p.   ) and index.
    1. Marriage—United States.   2. Afro-Americans—Marriage.
3. Afro-American women—Psychology.   4. Afro-American
men—Psychology.   5. Interpersonal relations—United States.
I. Hopson, Darlene Powell.   II. Title.   III. Title: Friends,
lovers, and soul mates.
HQ734.H83   1994
646.7'8'08996073—dc20   93-39327
                                                        CIP

ISBN 0-671-76837-9

God blessed us with ideal role models of a soul-mate relationship. Darlene's parents, Robert and Leanna Powell, will soon be married forty years and they still sustain a balance between their roles as friends, lovers, and partners. They show us that a happy marriage can endure the most challenging of times.

We were also fortunate to have grandparents who maintained strong relationships for more than fifty years, severed only by death of a partner:

> CONNIE AND LAURA POWELL
> WEST AND VESSIE HOPSON

And for their personal inspiration:

> *Uncle West and Aunt Lottie Hopson—*
> *married 50 years*
> *Uncle Phil and Aunt Jean Hopson—*
> *married 28 years*
> *Dear friends Milton and Sandra Maxwell—*
> *married 25 years*

ACKNOWLEDGMENTS

We extend a heartfelt thanks to our editor, Marilyn J. Abraham; editorial assistant, Dawn Marie Daniels; and our agent, Barbara Lowenstein, for their tireless commitment and support in bringing this book to fruition. We appreciated the editorial guidance and motivation they provided and the focus groups they organized. We would like especially to acknowledge the editorial assistance of Karyn Feiden, a New York–based author and coauthor of numerous books, including *Against the Odds: The Story of AIDS Drug Development, Politics and Profits*. Her assistance in transforming a somewhat unwieldy manuscript and much supplementary material into a well-organized, polished book was invaluable.

We would also like to express appreciation to our colleagues and dear brother/sister/friends, psychologists Dr. Thomas Parham and Dr. C. Aldrena Mabry for reading the final manuscript and providing insightful feedback. The collective sense of responsibility and cooperative spirit we all shared was inspirational.

We offer special thanks to all the individuals and couples who shared their stories with us, those in our clinical practice and those who are friends and colleagues. We have presented the information in a way that guarantees the confidentiality of our conversations. May this book be a source of guidance and inspiration in developing or enhancing a soul-mate relationship.

C O N T E N T S

10 ▲ CONTENTS

INTRODUCTION

Black American culture is built upon a foundation of strong kinship and community ties that can be traced back to our African origins. In the isolated villages from which our ancestors were torn, individual survival depended on the survival of the tribe. "I am because we are, and because we are, therefore, I am," wrote J. S. Mbiti in *African Religions and Philosophies*,[1] beautifully capturing the sense of interdependency that characterized African tribal life.

Through centuries of bondage, that sense of connection was sorely tested, first by the cruelties and enforced separations of slavery, later by racism, economic struggle, and misguided social welfare policies. Yet the love and loyalty within so many African-American families endured, becoming a mainstay of our existence in a hostile world.

Despite this proud heritage, there is a crisis of intimacy in the Black community. As practicing psychologists who specialize in marital and family therapy, we work daily with Black couples who are struggling to heal troubled love relationships. We also speak with single people who despair of ever finding suitable partners. We have grown alarmed at the distrust and hostility we are witnessing among Black men and women.

"Why are Black men such dogs?" asks a thirty-two-year-old fashion designer in despair.

"Why are Black women such bitches?" a forty-year-old sales manager demands to know.

Ugly questions, but they surface time and time again both in our clinical practice and in conversations with friends and colleagues. Black men and women sometimes seem to be at war with each other. "Like flowers struggling to bloom, Black male-female relationships are finding their roots to new growth being strangled by the weeds of selfishness, exploitation, deceit, faulty expectations, self-centeredness, poor timing, and sometimes bad luck," write our colleagues Joseph L. White and Thomas A. Parham in *The Psychology of Blacks*,[2] a groundbreaking exploration of that subject.

We believe it is time for a truce. We must set aside our weapons, tear down our defenses, confront our differences, and learn again how to liberate, preserve, and take pleasure in Black love. At a time when Black families are besieged by troubles that originate with racism and poverty, we must reclaim our heritage and the bonds of love that have allowed us to travel together thus far.

Although the problems of intimacy and commitment between Black men and women are not new, they have been discussed only in whispers and behind closed doors for too long. We have been reluctant to air interpersonal conflicts publicly, fearing that any admission of difficulties may be used to further divide our people. Some of our African-American brothers and sisters have believed it wiser to ignore mounting tensions than to risk divisive confrontations. Unfortunately, this tradition of keeping up appearances prevents us from exploring the sources of our grievances against one another and from learning the skills of constructive struggle and assertive communication that enable us to find common ground.

Novelist Terry McMillan broke important new ground for all of us with her bestselling novel *Waiting to Exhale*. By writing about the frustrations, disappointments, and challenges that Black women face in their search for Mr. Right, she helped open the door for candid discussion about issues of love between African-Americans. We believe *Friends, Lovers, and Soul Mates* will help fill the void Ms. McMillan exposed by providing the tools, direction, and support that African-Americans need to develop fully satisfying relationships.

The process of developing healthy relationships begins with confronting our concerns and committing ourselves to change. As our clients repeatedly demonstrate, psychological wounds, no matter how old, cannot heal unless they are openly acknowledged and directly addressed. Until we take a hard look at the combination of historical legacies, socioeconomic influences, and psychological factors that are forcing a wedge between Black men and women, we cannot expect healing to take place. This can be a painful process, but it is far better than perpetuating the vicious cycle of conflict, family disintegration, and community breakdown.

Are you looking for a special companion? Frustrated because you can't seem to communicate with the person you are with? Frightened by the shortage of Black men? Eager to find a woman who will accept you, blemishes and all? Tired of rehashing the same battles, night after night and year after year? Determined to meet someone whose vision matches yours? If so, *Friends, Lovers, and Soul Mates* is for you. We think the candid insights about the influences of your past and the concrete advice about communication and dealing with such sensitive subjects as money, family, sex, religion, and ethnic identity can change the way you approach intimacy.

Our interest in strengthening Black relationships emerges from our passionate commitment to help empower the Black community. We have counseled hundreds of men, women, couples, and families in the joint private psychotherapy practice we run in Middlefield, Connecticut. Among our other joint activities, we conduct youth-oriented workshops that focus on such topics as self-esteem, racial harmony, and preparing for the future, and write a monthly advice column for *YSB (Young Sisters and Brothers) Magazine*. Derek also counsels formerly incarcerated men and Darlene explores Black women's issues in the group therapy sessions she facilitates.

Although our psychology training and clinical experience have been invaluable, our knowledge also comes from the commitment we have made to our own marriage—eight years old and thriving—and from the shared tasks of raising two beautiful children and developing a growing business. Because we aspire to live by what we advocate, we devote a lot of energy to being introspective and scrutinizing ourselves and our communication styles and to modeling the most effective methods for confronting disagreement and reaching consensus.

We know through firsthand experience about the challenge of sustaining a positive and loving relationship in the face of personal differences, economic pressures, and racism. But we also know that the emotional, social, and sexual bonds that link Black men and women together can provide a safe haven in a stormy sea. There is no magic wand to create those nourishing bonds, no thirty-day formula to guarantee long-lasting love. A successful relationship requires ongoing review and purposeful effort. Our intention in writing *Friends, Lovers, and Soul Mates* is to convince you the effort is worth making.

PART I

▲ ▼ ▲ ▼

SETTING THE STAGE FOR LOVE

▲ ▼ ▲ ▼ ▲ ▼ ▲ ▼ ▲ ▼ ▲ ▼ ▲ ▼ ▲ ▼

What Is a
Soul Mate?

▲ ▼

Soul mates have a special place in the lives of Black people in contemporary American society because they allow us to shed the burdens we carry through the day. In the safe haven created by intimacy, we find a place to speak honestly about ourselves and to heal from the wounds inflicted on us. Most of us are happiest when we have the opportunity to love and be loved; most of us thrive in the close bonds of commitment. As one of our clients said to his girlfriend, "When the world is kicking me and I'm down, it is you whom I look to for support. And I'd like to be able to do the same thing for you."

If you are fortunate, you may have known some intimate couples whose love has endured through times of trouble and times of joy. Their loyalty, support, and commitment to each other have not flagged, even when the circumstances of their lives have changed. They may share common interests, laugh at the same jokes, have similar taste in movies, and travel well together. When conflicts surface, they negotiate their differences in a climate of trust. They feel safe taking emotional risks, knowing they will not be attacked for admitting vulnerabilities. They are often sexually adventurous and committed to fidelity. Each feels comfortable with his or her own racial and spiritual identity and each partner respects the other's differences. Like all couples, they surely have their trials, but even when they disagree or disappoint each other, they avoid becoming bitter or accusatory. In all of their dealings, they find ways to uplift each other and to infuse hope and determination into the hardships of daily life.

But perhaps you have not had the privilege of knowing such inspirational soul mates. Perhaps your parents quarreled constantly as each one sought to gain the upper hand. Or your father was absent altogether and your mother went from one bad relationship to another. You may have been raised by adults who did not readily express emotions or who vented their frustrations on each other. Perhaps you were smothered and overprotected. Maybe your parents were emotionally distant. You may even have been emotionally, physically, or sexually abused.

Most likely you are still paying the price for these childhood experiences. The absence of strong, positive role models almost always leaves scars, and as an adult, you will have to struggle to resolve the experiences of a painful past. If intimacy was unfamiliar to you, you may be so fearful of getting close to other people that you sabotage your own relationships. Or perhaps the emotional void created in childhood was so intense that you scare potential partners away with your feverish efforts to get close. Men and women who grew up without healthy role models may also create unrealistic fantasies about an ideal lover—and then find it hard to understand why no one meets their expectations.

Whatever your particular experiences, the result is likely to be the same—you can't find love or you can't hold on to it when you do. A traditional Buddhist aphorism identifies at least part of the solution to your troubles: When the student is ready, the teacher appears. Essentially the same thing can be said for a soul mate. When you have developed a secure sense of your own identity, worked through some of the unresolved conflicts of childhood, feel confident and happy with yourself, and are receptive to a serious relationship, you are ready at last to make a commitment to a special person.

Rachel and Bill have the type of soul-mate relationship that many men and women, married or single, are seeking. Through a forty-year marriage that endured some terrible moments, they nurtured a powerful, intimate, and inspiring connection. When the winds of racism began to blow in their small Arkansas town, Bill headed north to Chicago in search of work; two years passed before Rachel and their children could join him. A decade later their son was killed in a tragic accident and the couple drew close to sustain each other through the terrible pain. Bill was involved in a brief but tempestuous affair and Rachel struggled with temptation, although she eventually decided to resist the advances of a family friend.

Over the years, they have also shared some moments of magic. They cherish six healthy grandchildren, have paid a triumphant visit to their ancestral homeland in the Ivory Coast, and won a community service award for developing innovative programs for inner-city youngsters. In their toughest times and at moments that shined most brightly, Rachel and Bill always valued their love and respect for each other.

The remarkable thing about such soul mates is that they light up everyone around them with the depth of their feelings. A day spent in their presence can be a day spent in serenity. In *Beloved*, Nobel Prize–winner Toni Morrison's extraordinary novel about love and loss, a slave named Sixo captured the power of a soul-mate connection when he describes his relationship with the Thirty-Mile Woman, named for the distance he'd walk in each direction for the chance to spend an hour with her. Sixo declares: "She is a friend of mine. She gather me, man. The pieces I am, she gather them and give them back to me in all the right order.

It's good, you know, when you got a woman who is a friend of your mind." Such is the potential for Black love.

THE LOVE WE SEEK

What sort of person can create this type of bond with you? Who is willing to understand and accept you as you are? Who can create a safe space where you feel protected from the often-painful realities of being an African-American in this society?

Our discussions with hundreds of Black men and women over the years have helped us identify some highly valued soul-mate characteristics. There's no shopping list of ingredients, of course, and obviously everyone has differing priorities. Needs also change over time—it may be important to find a brother with a good-looking body when you are twenty-one, while financial stability and the willingness to commit often become more significant by the time you reach thirty-five. Some women are also discovering that Black men with solid values and respectable, but not glamorous, jobs—the mail carriers, bus drivers, and office clerks they may once have written off as less than they deserve—can be worthy and loving mates.

What Black Men Want

Imagine how Black men might be in a world with fewer obstacles and more support. What if we could eliminate the negative images that have been created, not only in the minds of White people but, tragically, in our own minds as well? Haki R. Madhubuti, the poet, essayist, and literary critic, offers this stirring description in his essay "Black Manhood: Toward a Definition":

> a lover of life and all that is beautiful. one who is constantly growing and who learns from mistakes. a challenger of the known and the unknown. the first to admit that he does not

know as he seeks to find out. able to solicit the best out of self and others. soft. strong. not afraid to take the lead. creative father. organized and organizer. a brother to brothers. a brother to sisters. understanding. patient. a winner. maintainer of the i can, i must, i will attitude toward Black struggle and life. a builder of the necessary. always and always in a process of growth and without a doubt believes that our values and traditions are not negotiable.[1]

With Madhubuti's ideal in mind, let us try to answer the question our sisters keep asking: What does the Black man want from his woman?

She needs to let me admit my need for compassion. Media stereotypes depict Black men as hard and dangerous and our own pride makes us want to convey an image of emotional strength. But the truth is that we confront a cold world every day and want to find some warmth, comfort, and compassion from the women we love. We don't want to be fawned over but we want to be able to let our guard down and have our feelings affirmed. One of our clients puts it like this: "When things are rough, I want to make sure my woman can be a friend to me. I want to be able to talk to her and know that she will be there for me."

In the African tradition, we have a saying that "life at its best is a creative synthesis of opposites in fruitful harmony." Taken literally, it tells us that a Black man may discover his own strengths in moments of great vulnerability. But it takes a supportive and loving woman to see that strength.

She should be comfortable with her own sexuality. Many Black men tell us they are looking for a woman who is sensual and at ease with her sexuality. Some adjectives they use to describe this blend are well groomed, attractive, affectionate, attentive, and responsive. But the stereotype that men are just "looking for a little piece of action" doesn't hold up. In our discussion groups, men say having an orgasm isn't enough to achieve full sexual satisfaction. "Sure, the physical release is important, but so are the emotions that go along with it," said a young attorney. If a woman is uptight or unresponsive, it is difficult to connect with her emotionally.

She should know how to be strong without being hostile. The painful history that has forced Black women to be strong has been a great asset to our families and our communities, but some men feel that women are confusing strength with combativeness. "If her being strong means that we have to fight all the time, then I have a problem with that," said one man, complaining about women who approach relationships as if they are arming for battle. "I don't think a woman has to prove that she is always right to be liberated." He termed his own goal "egalitarian intimacy": "I see us as companions and equal partners, two adults who are going forth and sharing ourselves. I'm not interested in either one of us baby-sitting the other." Women have to be careful not to confuse assertiveness with aggression that may be displaced from earlier, failed relationships.

She should take pride in her ethnic identity and spiritual roots. Men who have a strong sense of themselves as African-Americans often feel that women with similar outlooks can better understand the travails of a Black man's existence in this society. A spiritual foundation, which has historically been central to the lives of our people, also remains important to many men. When it comes to both ethnicity and spirituality, the key to compatibility is not being perfectly matched but feeling comfortable with differences.

She should not have a hidden agenda. Men resent women who bring a set of rigid expectations to their relationship, especially when they aren't candid about them. There's nothing more frustrating than discovering you are being tested or judged without your knowledge. "If you want something from me, come right out and ask for it," pleaded one man at a session we set up to explore the sources of gender conflict.

Men also complain about women who play games, such as flirting with no intention of becoming sexually involved or being deliberately outrageous to provoke a reaction. And they resent being judged by standards they consider irrelevant—mainstream society, for example, tends to define manhood in terms of financial resources or control over other people, achievements that have little value in a true Afrocentric relationship. "Some women make me feel like I should submit a résumé," said an insurance broker named Stan. "They want to know right away about my job, my paycheck, even my bank account. Those are ugly-acting sisters and I try to stay away from them."

She's got to trust me. A common complaint from Black men is that their women don't trust them to have nonsexual friendships or business dealings with other women. They feel that their romantic partners view them through a lens of suspicion, assuming they are likely to stray off course unless they are constrained by a tight leash. In one of our discussions, a radio producer described his irritation when his girlfriend kept questioning him about a friendship that dated back to his teenage years. "I felt that I was being nagged unfairly. I don't lie to my woman. If I say she is my friend, I need to be trusted about that. I don't want to be in a position where I have to justify having lunch with someone."

She shouldn't put me down. Black men often have a heightened fear of appearing weak or dominated, especially by women. Because of the way they are treated in White society, they are extremely sensitive to perceived threats against their manhood and often bristle if they feel they are being criticized or ordered around. "I want a woman who builds me up, not someone who tears me down," said one man. Men who are struggling to become more assertive and to deal more effectively with the battering impact of racism want encouraging support, not negativity and nagging. They also want women to realize that their visions of success may differ and that they shouldn't be criticized for those differences.

What Black Women Want

Today's Black woman is complex and multifaceted. She is strong, but sometimes wants a man she can lean on. She can take care of herself but doesn't always want to have to do so. She values a brother who is sensitive, who believes in himself, and who can distinguish between assertiveness and hostility. With thanks to Haki Madhubuti,[2] we have borrowed the "Black Manhood" essay as a guide for our own portrait of Black sisters at their best:

> a giver of life and all that is splendid. one who learns from the past as she journeys down new paths towards the future. a planter, an explorer, a singer of songs. open to ideas from others. loving and loveable. strong. beautiful. soft and gentle. supportive and nurturing. attentive and caring. a sister to sisters. a sister to brothers. devoted mother. empathetic. assertive and resourceful. carrier and keeper of the culture, at all times believing i can, we can, we must. loyal to family, committed to community. victorious. eternally dedicated to the upliftment of her people.

Like the men, Black women obviously have differing needs. Still, our clinical practice and personal experiences have given us some insight into the question we are so often asked: What do Black women want?

He's got to tell the truth. Honesty is at the top of most lists and the ability to talk about sensitive and personal subjects is typically considered a must. "I don't want my man to play games with me, I want him to be honest," one woman told us. "If we can't be real, nothing else is going to make up for that." Whether the topic is dating other people, making a commitment, feeling blue, or shaping a vision of the future, women want to be able to communicate frankly with their men.

He needs to let me know that he loves me. Openly expressed affection is important to many. "I don't want to guess whether a man loves me, I want to know," said a client named Freddie. "Otherwise, I'm always holding back, afraid to give too much. I want to feel free to be as loving as I can be." We asked Freddie what gave her confidence that she was loved, and she emphasized small considerations—a man who fulfills commitments, calls to say he'll be late, stays attuned to her feelings, and asks questions about her day. "It's the little, everyday things that show he really cares."

He needs to know who he is. Women who have clearly defined goals and a systematic strategy for pursuing them often value stability and a sense of direction. "I want a man who can say, 'This is who I am, this is what I want, this is how I'm going after it,' " said the owner of a small business. "The avenue he pursues doesn't matter, just so he is clear about himself." Black women who include professional achievements and financial stability as criteria for a soul mate often say they are not so much concerned about the size of a man's paycheck as the health of his ego— they feel that someone who likes his job is more likely to have the sense of accomplishment that is crucial to self-esteem.

He's got to have some sense of spirituality. African-American women who turn to spirituality for hope and inspiration, in good times and in bad, usually look for men who respect the power of worship, meditation, or prayer. Although she does not attend formal church services, Margaret considers herself quite spiritual and says she needs a man who feels the same way: "If my partner appreciates a higher power, we can tap into faith together and in that way find inspiration and replenish our souls."

He's got to give something back to the Black community. Many women who are upwardly mobile and at ease in main-stream, White society still feel deeply committed to strengthening the lot of those who have been left behind and they want their partners to feel the same way. "That doesn't mean that he has to march in every demonstration or make Black power the focus of his life," said one woman as clarification. "But he has to be proud of and aware of his African identity. Someone who is in denial about it or doesn't think it is important would not be the right person for me." Whether a man forges links to the Black community through his spiritual beliefs, his artistic passions, or his political concerns, her notion is that he give back. "I want him to have a sense of something larger than himself in the world."

He needs to respect my talents. Many Black women are proud of their professional accomplishments, often achieved by a great amount of talent and drive and usually against numerous obstacles. They want to be involved with a man who respects them and has the confidence not to feel threatened by their success. And they want the space to keep on growing. As one woman told us: "I don't want to be in a relationship that is all-consuming. A man's got to know where he begins and where I begin. He doesn't try to take me away from myself."

He shouldn't try to control me. Many African-American women bristle when they feel that men are trying to dictate their behavior or deny them an autonomous identity. This is especially true of younger women who are just beginning to define a firm sense of self. As one aspiring model told us: "I want someone who can just allow me to be me. There's an awful lot of guys out there who think they can tell you what to do, what to wear, and who your friends should be. That gets old real fast."

He should bolster my self-esteem. Everyone has insecurities, and psychologically healthy women look for partners who are reassuring and supportive, not men whose main way of relating is to put them down. A shy young woman explained why this matters to her. "I want someone who will help me cultivate my better qualities. I tend to be introverted so I look for someone who likes being out there, someone who will encourage my efforts to become more assertive."

He should consider my needs. A common complaint among women is that their men are self-centered and listen carelessly, if they listen at all. "It's always about them," complained one woman. "Even when we are talking about feelings, some guys only want to know how I feel about *them*, not how I feel in general." Black women are hungry for relationships in which their men pay attention, express interest and concern, and encourage discussion. These efforts extend into the sexual arena— Black women want it understood that they enjoy good sex and expect to have their needs met. "My man needs to realize the time we spend in bed is not just time for him to be taking care of himself," one woman told us. "He's got to know he is also there for my pleasure."

SELF-ASSESSMENT EXERCISE: THE SOUL MATE OF YOUR DREAMS

While these generalizations are useful, it also helps to identify the characteristics that especially matter to you. Is your ideal lover a lady who operates smoothly in just about any social circle? A man who is the life of every party? Someone who is deeply involved with African-American causes? How important are education, financial achievement, and professional interests? What about family ties and a spiritual connection?

To establish your personal priorities, rank the importance of the following statements, giving each one a score between 1 and 10:

10   9   8   7   6   5   4   3   2   1

Very   Not important
important   at all

We both have a strong sense of ethnic identity.
We share a common vision of the future.
We are emotionally intimate and can share feelings.
We are intellectually compatible.
We are faithful to each other.
The sex is really hot.

We have attained similar educational levels.
We are each willing to make sacrifices for the other.
We maintain independent friendships outside this relation-
  ship.
I am physically attracted to him/her.
He/she feels closely tied to the Black church.
He/she has strong spiritual values.
He/she tries to give something back to the Black community.
He/she is comfortable "switching up" in White circles.
He/she has a professionally satisfying career.
He/she makes a lot of money.
My family approves of the match.
We communicate openly and honestly.
He/she has a great body.
We explore new ways to please each other sexually.
He/she is romantic.
We share concerns and feelings.
He/she talks to me about the past and about hopes for the
  future.
He/she believes in family.

Now divide these statements in two, putting anything you ranked
6 or above in one group. These tell you a lot about the characteristics that really matter to you. Anything ranking below 5 is
probably not very important and may even be a characteristic
that makes you feel uncomfortable.

Review both groups to help you assess whether the person you
are dating, or the one you are looking for, is right for you. Consider whether you are attracted by superficial or enduring qualities. Remember, relationships don't usually last if they are based
solely on external factors—good looks, lots of money, and hot
sex can be real turn-ons but if these change, the basis of your
compatibility may be gone. Internal emotional qualities, such as

compassion, trustworthiness, and a strong sense of self-esteem, usually endure and provide the foundation for true intimacy.

ABOUT HEALTHY STRUGGLE

Of course, there is a lot more to falling in love than meeting the man or woman who fits a fantasy profile. For one thing, there's an amorphous quality called "attraction" that cannot be ignored. We don't believe in the myths of real love without effort, mutual respect without sacrifice, or passion without balance, but we do think that relationships between Black men and women are too special to settle for a match that "makes sense" but just doesn't feel right.

In one of our discussion groups, a financial consultant named Tanya talked about the good-looking architect she almost married. "He made a good salary and was eager to make a commitment. All the ingredients were right and my family was telling me I should go for it." Tanya felt that she was ready to settle down and tried to convince herself that the architect was a true soul mate, but she could not pretend to an excitement she did not really feel. "He was the right guy according to what society says is important but he just didn't make it for me. The chemistry wasn't there."

Tanya was content to remain single until she met the right partner, and she may well have been wise in allowing her heart to rule her head—marriages based entirely on practical considerations are seldom happy. On the other hand, relationships that endure have to be grounded in realistic expectations. One reason so many Black men and women find it difficult to sustain lasting intimacy is that they are operating with many misconceptions about love. Thanks in part to Hollywood films and celebrity magazines, many of us still believe, perhaps at a less than fully conscious level, in fairy-tale encounters and magical connections. Perhaps you are expecting lightning to strike when Mr.

Right walks through the door for the first time. Maybe you are waiting for a love connection so intense, so spontaneous, and so harmonious that no effort will ever be required to sustain it.

If so, we've got some startling news: Most soul-mate relationships aren't born that way and they certainly won't last unless attitudes change. The truth is that preserving a meaningful relationship takes effort, discipline, and sacrifice. Connections that last involve a commitment to "work on loving" through direct, assertive, conscious, and purposeful efforts.

In healthy relationships, Black couples who stay together never stop growing emotionally, through struggle and commitment. As they grapple with the disappointments, the frustration, and sometimes the anguish that are a part of life, they strive not to displace anger onto those they love. They also search for the internal fortitude that helps them avoid being demoralized by racism or bogged down by the personal deficits that have their origins in unhappy childhood experiences and human frailty. They are available to each other both sensually and sexually, and their ability to display vulnerability to each other provides a special and splendid level of intimacy.

Learning to communicate effectively and to compromise fairly is a lifelong process. Even at moments when it feels safer to keep your thoughts to yourself, love demands candor. One element that all soul-mate relationships have in common is that they are not a place in which to hide; rather, they are a place in which to be revealed. If there is a single message we try to convey to our clients, our friends, and our colleagues, it is this: *Intimacy is impossible when communication is blocked; intimacy flourishes when communication flows smoothly.*

Genuine soul mates spend most of their energy engaged in productive struggle, not in hurtful battles. The challenge of sustaining any soul-mate relationship is to constantly replenish the reservoir of love with waters that soothe and invigorate. Occasionally, clients come into our office asking us, essentially, to "fix" them. Therapy, of course, can do no such thing. What we try to do instead, in our counseling practice, in group discussions, and in this book, is to encourage Black men and women to accept responsibility for their own growth. This involves working on their relationships with themselves, with each other, and with their community. We also try to instill hope and to serve as role models for people wondering whether to take the risk of making changes. In the process, we emphasize the need for soul mates to support each other—the phrase we like is: "Don't criticize, *energize.*"

As you strive for intimacy, remember the following commandments and honor them as best you can:

Do some work on yourself. The path toward intimacy begins with an honest look at yourself. It is easy to become so caught up in the struggles of daily life that you forget to reflect fully on who you are and how you got that way. Periods of introspection and self-assessment are crucial for personal development. The more you understand your own strengths and weaknesses, your likes and dislikes, your values and vision, the greater the insights you will gain into others. Keeping God first in your life allows you to love yourself and this will enable you to love others.

Keep your eyes on the prize. We are convinced that finding and sustaining a relationship is a worthwhile pursuit. Believe in yourself and your ability to control your own destiny and to resolve conflicts. Stay focused on your vision of a mutually nourishing bond when the waters in which you are sailing turn muddy, and soon enough you will move into clearer seas.

Try a little tenderness. Whether you are dating casually or celebrating a golden anniversary, never stop respecting your partner. Be gentle with each other. A soul-mate relationship is not the place to be adversarial. Believe in each other, offer a supporting hand, not a critical eye, and remember that African-

Americans have always valued individual sacrifice in the interest of a collective vision. Seek to inspire those you love.

Look for common ground. Try to bend in your relationships. Flexibility and the willingness to emphasize similarities, rather than differences, are essential ingredients of conflict resolution. Learn to negotiate your differences. We struggle enough with issues of power and control in the workplace; keep the home an amicable place where compromise is not mistaken for defeat.

Let the flames burn on. At times the fire that fuels your love may die down to a spark. Be mindful about adding new logs from time to time so that the flame is not extinguished. Soul mates need to be more than business partners to each other. Although shared work can enrich intimacy, a committed relationship also involves bonds of friendship and romance. Take time to laugh and play together, to enjoy moments of passion, to exchange small gifts, and to discuss the week's events.

To thine own self be true. Although genuine love involves teamwork and sacrifice, it does not require either partner to shed a sense of self. To the contrary: Interdependence is bolstered when both partners also focus on their own development. By maintaining your individuality and nurturing your other friendships, you both have new experiences to share that keep a relationship fresh.

Keep the faith. Don't get caught up in Hollywood myths about perfect relationships, sex that is always intense, and communication that is never less than totally candid. There will be times when you are not at your best. Inevitably, you may sometimes become frustrated or angry with your mate. There's no such thing as lovers who don't quarrel. When times get rough, have confidence that things will improve. Be willing to make the first move to get your relationship moving in a positive direction. Have faith: The best may be yet to come.

Heritage: Africa and the American Experience

▲ ▼

The story of African-Americans is as much one of endurance as of tragedy. Throughout the centuries of physical and mental bondage that began when we were yanked from our homeland by slave traders, the heart and the soul of the African-American people have never been destroyed. We have been blessed with resilient ancestors who found ways to stay alive, to keep tradition intact, and, despite extraordinary adversity, to preserve family ties. The tale of our survival can be a source of inspiration as we begin the journey toward a soul-mate relationship.

It may seem odd to encounter a sketch of Black history in a book about love, but as psychologists, we believe that delving into the past is the first step toward claiming the future. If you are sitting home on a Saturday night without a date, perhaps it is hard to understand why it matters. When you are overwhelmed by loneliness, frustrated by another lovers' quarrel, or inflamed by the discovery of infidelity, the lives of your ancestors may not feel especially relevant. But history has a direct influence on how we view ourselves and, as a result, on how we relate to others. If we do not know where we came from, we cannot fully understand where we are today or the direction in which we are headed. Only by recognizing the influence of the past on our lives today can we begin at last to gain control over our own destiny.

WHY AFRICA MATTERS

In recent years, many Black people have returned to the wellspring of tradition to draw nourishment. Some have traveled to ancestral homes in West Africa to retrace family connections; others have plunged into the study of African civilization. Many have also been active in encouraging their school districts to adopt an Afrocentric or multicultural curriculum.

Whatever route we choose, we are finding that digging at our African roots uncovers rich traditions, such as collectivism, spirituality, openness, and loyalty, that can help us rebuild our most intimate relationships and our communities. Learning more about our homeland also reminds us that we are descended from a strong and proud people whose blood still runs through our veins. To this day, their voice shines through in our music and our art, in the stories we tell, and in the literature we write. It is a voice that sustains us with its determined and spirited life force and testifies to our ability to survive and to a spirit that has never been broken.

In Africa, and later in the United States, our people survived because in their most difficult moments they remained united, uplifting, and inspiring with one another. The more we understand the strengths that kept us whole, the better able we are to draw upon them as we search for love and ways to hold on to it.

Although European slave traffickers advanced the myth that Africans were savage, primitive people, ours was actually an advanced society many centuries before Europe began to emerge from its medieval period. The dominant allegiance of our ancestors was to the tribe, an organism with many faces but a single set of shared goals. The concerns of the community, not those of its individual members, were the focus of every decision; collective survival was the objective underlying tradition. Ours was an expressive culture that used dance, music, and ritual celebrations to speak of compassion, love, joy, and sensuality. We respected the land and felt connected to all that surrounded us. Because all members of our tribe were part of a chain linking us both to our ancestors and to our unborn children, the alienation that pervades Western culture today was largely unknown.

The strong, interconnected kinship networks that thrived in Africa imposed rights and responsibilities on their members in exchange for social and economic security. There are lessons in this collective approach that apply directly to our lives today and to our efforts to strengthen Black relationships. The African model teaches us that we have a shared purpose and must care for each other as we would care for ourselves. Only by approaching each other with the spirit of unity that has existed for centuries in Africa, and not as enemies, can we find common ground.

Generally speaking, African societies viewed marriage not only as the joining of one man with one woman but as a means of linking two extended families to expand their influence as an economic, religious, and political unit. Marriages could be arranged by the prospective partners or by their kin; in either case, all parties had to consent before the ceremony took place. After marriage, a couple usually lived together in an existing family compound typically comprised of a series of adjoining dwellings.

Today the traditions of the extended family remain intact. Strong kinship ties enrich many of our emotional lives and often provide a source of practical support as well. Many of us rely on relatives to help us as we start our married lives. By baby-sitting, offering us a home while we save for the down payment to buy our own, or providing a hot meal when we need one, they uplift our spirits and ease pressures that can interfere with soul-mate intimacy.

Conflicts sometimes arise when one partner has been raised within the structure of an extended family while another grew up in a nuclear family. Wanda and Sam sought marital counseling after Wanda took in two nephews because her sister was entering a drug-treatment program. Wanda, who had herself been raised by her grandmother and an aunt, had not hesitated when her sister made the request; her kinship ties taught her this was simply how things were done. Sam, who had never had especially close connections to extended family, seethed with resentment. He viewed the youngsters as an intrusion, feared the loss of his privacy, and was concerned about the impact on their daughter.

We found it extremely productive to help Sam and Wanda appreciate the historical context of their struggle. We encouraged Sam to consider that Wanda's family loyalties were rooted in thousands of years of African tradition and helped Wanda realize that Sam's perspective reflected a common, contemporary family structure in American society. These insights did not provide an instant solution to their conflict but they heightened mutual awareness. Rather than blame each other, Sam and Wanda were able to see that the other person had a valid point of view, which made it easier to talk honestly about feelings.

In Africa monogamy was the norm, but long ago, in some regions, it was accepted practice for a man to have two or more wives. This is one of the legacies of our past that remind us that while the African model can be inspiring, it does not offer an ideal that can be imitated blindly. Sometimes we hear brothers trying to justify their present-day infidelity with references to older African traditions, but we suspect this is usually just an excuse for self-centered behavior. We'll be talking more about the meaning and value of commitment and monogamy in later chapters.

When children were born in Africa, they were tended both by

parents and by other kin. Aunts and uncles were expected to assume certain responsibilities, and grandparents, who were viewed as the vital links between the past and the present, held positions of special influence and honor. Within a family compound, all children were considered brothers and sisters; the distinction between cousins and siblings was largely irrelevant. Men were intimately involved with their children, especially their sons, to whom they passed down the crucial survival skills of warrior, hunter, and carpenter. Now, as then, children remain at the center of family life as we struggle to improve conditions for the next generation and to pass down our enduring heritage.

THE AMERICAN EXPERIENCE

Despite the rich African legacy, experiences in the United States have cast a long shadow over our lives. If Africa has been a fountain of strength, the American experience has often been a source of great sorrow. Although many of our people have achieved success, it is impossible to address the crisis of intimacy among Black Americans without reference to our cruel past. We know how difficult it is to help adults learn to like themselves and to trust other people if they have been abused as children. When an entire race has been mistreated in much the same way, reclaiming the God-given right of love poses even greater challenges.

Right now, Black women are asking: "What is wrong with Black men?" and Black men want to know: "What is wrong with Black women?" Instead of berating each other, we should also ask: "How have African-Americans been wronged?" The goal is not to place blame but to understand the obstacles that must be overcome to find love. Although we believe the power to make constructive changes rests in our hands, our current plight has not been entirely of our own making. There is nothing inherently flawed about our people.

• • •

Three harsh facts distinguish the history of Black Americans in the United States. First, we were snatched from our African homes, violently severed from our families, and brought to this country in chains. No other immigrant group endured the same indignities. Many ancient kinship bonds were shattered as the slave ships sailed from the shores of West Africa.

Secondly, we were transported to a world whose values and traditions were radically different from our own. From our homeland, where tribal allegiances and collective decision making shaped our lives, we came to a nation structured around individualism and entrepreneurship.

Finally, once by law and later by custom, we have been denied the rights and privileges awarded to White people in American society. The resulting economic and social pressures fostered further family fragmentation.

Every time a Black man and a Black woman come together today and wonder whether their love can endure, their individual experiences are clouded by the past. As enslaved persons, we had very little control over our own lives; we were told that we were not worthy of freedom and denied the right to shape our destiny. Later, our oppressors argued that Black brains were physiologically inferior to White brains. To this day, we are continually sent messages that say: "You are Black and therefore there are certain things you are not capable of doing." The ordeals of our history linger in the collective memory and contribute to a sense of inadequacy, low self-esteem, and feelings of inferiority. The long-term psychological consequences of racism can make us feel unworthy of good fortune and cause us to doubt ourselves and our capacity for love. As a result, it becomes harder to trust others or to take the risks necessary to deepen soul-mate bonds.

Black author Na'im Akbar describes oppression as an unnatural phenomenon that results in unnatural human behavior and inevitably distorts relationships. In his insightful book *Chains and*

Images of Psychological Slavery,[1] Akbar helps us understand how oppression and dehumanization have damaged the African-American psyche and led to a loss of self-respect.

To repair Black relationships, we must not only examine personal and family issues but also confront and process our history so that it loses its power over our lives. Only then are we free to declare: "I am a beautiful Black person and there is nothing I cannot do." When we have internalized this belief, we are ready to love ourselves and one another.

THE TRAGIC LEGACY OF SLAVERY

Slavery had a calamitous impact on our cultural heritage and our interpersonal relationships. Over a period of four centuries, European traders captured more than ten million Africans and exported them as human commodities to South America, the Caribbean, and the United States. The cries of women who begged to be taken into captivity in exchange for their children's freedom went largely unheeded. In the ultimate betrayal, some of our Black brothers and sisters made common cause with the White man to sell their own kind into slavery, a tragic reminder that divisions within our ranks imperil our survival.

When the slave ships docked, our ancestors were alone in an alien culture. In a stark symbol of their lost identity, they were stripped of their African surnames and assigned new ones at the whim of their owners. Small wonder that, to this day, we are still struggling to understand who we are.

Young males, the warriors and hunters of Africa, were the prize of the slave traders; on some plantations men outnumbered women nine to one. But once in the New World the very masculinity that made them such sought-after raw material was stripped away. At this time, Black men began to learn a lesson that still creates relationship conflicts: Aggressive behavior is punished severely; to be docile is to survive.

That message has been handed down from father to son for generations and many of our brothers have grown up thinking that their survival depends on being submissive. Others have overcompensated to prove their masculinity by aggressive and hostile behavior toward society, toward Black women, and even toward each other. The result is that contemporary Black women sometimes feel frustrated because they cannot find an assertive man. The men they meet seem either too passive or too aggressive.

The absence of respect for marriage and family during the years of slavery left deep scars. Marriage between Black slaves had no formal legal standing and families were torn apart at will. Owners were considered the head of every slave household and could withhold permission for a marriage or insist that one occur. Sexual abuse was commonplace—it was the owner's prerogative to demand favors at whim. In many cases, Black men today are still paying a psychological price for feelings of inadequacy generated by the inability to protect their families and provide economic security. In our practice, we see this expressed in the avoidance of commitment and the adoption of self-centered attitudes that result in infidelity or the unwillingness to sacrifice for the greater good of a soul-mate relationship.

The slave master's lash has left its mark in other ways as well. By wrenching husbands from wives and severing the connection between parents and their children, slavery fostered the rootlessness that still plagues us. By stripping our people of their cultural ties, it destroyed the foundation of our lives and prevented us from building a new one. By denying men any means of protecting their families, it wounded our self-esteem.

That was apparent when we began counseling Keith and Janet. This professional couple came to us because Janet had given Keith an ultimatum: Stop getting involved with other women or I'm walking out. During our discussions, Keith told us that he wanted to stay married but said that agreeing to be sexually faithful felt to him like agreeing to be only half a man. We probed Keith's past to learn the origins of this attitude and discovered a family tradition of infidelity that led him to internalize the notion that a real man was a "stud" with many sexual partners.

The Black-men-as-studs image was fostered during slavery, when they were often forced to father children by many different women. Strong, good-looking men were considered desirable breeders who earned special favors from their owners. In the generations that followed, many men have continued to see having multiple sexual partners as proof of their desirability. This message has generated special enthusiasm among Black men who have not found other personal or professional ways to feel good about themselves. Because they feel financially impotent, they express their potency through sexual dominance instead.

Keith admitted that his adulterous affairs made him feel desirable, but he was intrigued by the connections that could be drawn between his behavior and the circumstances of slavery. By viewing the issue in its broader context, he saw that fidelity was actually a powerful expression of manhood, not a sign of weakness. As Keith opened himself more to feel Janet's pain, he realized that it sometimes takes more courage to resist sexual temptation than to yield to it.

Despite the tyranny of slavery, many African-Americans refused to accept defeat. History is rich with stories of enslaved persons who toiled from dawn to dusk, then scrubbed clothes through the night to earn pennies with which to purchase freedom—for themselves or for beloved parents, spouses, children, or siblings. Husbands fought desperately to protect their wives, parents struggled to spare their children. To the extent that it was possible, the African principles of mutual responsibility governed the daily lives of kin, and the extraordinary cooperation among many enslaved households helped ease the pain of childbirth, lighten the burdens of child rearing, and calm the fears of families expecting to be wrenched apart. Our ancestors demonstrated courage, determination, and a passionate commitment to family, the same characteristics soul mates strive for today.

From their inspiring stories of survival, we are reminded that the strength to rise above the indignities and limitations imposed by others ultimately lies within ourselves. If we are hated, we need not hate. If we are abused, we need not abuse ourselves or others. Instead of internalizing our experience of mistreatment, which makes us feel worthless and unlovable, we can reject its control over us. By emphasizing the strengths of our history, rather than its liabilities, we learn to focus on our own strengths. In the process, we empower ourselves and others as well.

FREE AT LAST?

The years that followed slavery have been bittersweet. At the time of Emancipation, newly freed slaves owned nothing but their own bodies—a significant advance, to be sure, but still far from enough. Few knew how to read and write. Some clung desperately to their plantations, working as little more than indentured servants because they knew no other life in the New World. Others wandered penniless, homeless, and bewildered through a region that was still in the grip of their enemies.

Yet in the midst of terrible hardships, they exploded the myth that all kinship ties had been destroyed and once again demonstrated astounding resilience. Soon after the Civil War ended, Southern roadways became clogged with Blacks moving from town to town in search of loved ones from whom they had been forcibly separated. There was a jamboree of family reunions, and our ancestors jumped the broom in great numbers to give legal standing to their slave vows. Historians say stable marriages became the norm, a finding that defies the recurring claim that Black family life did not survive slavery.

But it was many decades before Blacks found a political voice. In the early postslavery years, Black folks relied instead on inner strength, steadfast determination, and spiritual and kinship ties, tools that sustain us to this day. It was generally safer to swallow one's pride than to respond to racist insults, which sometimes made men feel less than whole. Derek's grandmother told us about an incident that occurred in 1919, soon after she and Derek's grandfather had moved north from Georgia. They were walking down a city street when a White man whistled at her and began making lewd remarks. Derek's grandfather wanted to confront the man and demand an apology but his wife restrained him. She later told us, "I knew that if he got involved in a fight, he'd be the one to get arrested. He was trembling with rage but I held his arm and pleaded with him to calm down and disregard the ignorant remarks. The experience was terribly frustrating and enraging for him because he felt he could not defend or protect me."

Eventually, anger and the determination to compel change began to replace acceptance. In the 1950s and 1960s, the civil rights and Black Power movements blasted open the doors of possibility. As we began to assert ourselves, the conscience of a nation gradually awakened.

Over the next fifteen years, the Black community built coalitions and made its voice heard at the highest levels of national power. African-Americans empowered themselves as never before. Instead of allowing others to control our lives, we took responsibility for correcting the wrongs that had been done to us. With memories of our ancestor's struggle, we began to fight back. Most of us stopped listening to the racist voices telling us we were worthless and began tuning into the brothers and sisters who said we could achieve great things. Some of us took the sentiments of the Black Power movement to heart. We internalized the message that "Black is beautiful" and began to see the physical beauty in our own people. Respect for ourselves, and a growing appreciation for our own culture, allowed us to make great strides, personally as well as politically.

Today, the hope that once burned with such fervor in the Black community has cooled. Despite the passion with which we have struggled against racism, it still pervades the communities where we live and shop, the schools our children attend, and the workplace. Too many of our people spoke the rhetoric of the Black Power movement but never fully internalized the words in order to sustain the changes.

Although the existence of a sizable Black middle and upper class gives us reason to be proud, a swelling Black underclass has been left behind without decent housing, affordable health care, adequate education, meaningful job opportunities, or reason to hope. Conditions have deteriorated for many of our brothers and sisters since the dawn of the civil rights movement. Most of the social ills plaguing this country affect our communities with special intensity and eat away at interpersonal relationships and family life. The recession and conservative backlash of recent years have only worsened the Black plight.

None of us are immune to the resulting tragedies. Even if we are part of the middle class, we may still have members of our extended families living in impoverished inner cities. Many of us are only a generation out of some of the nation's most neglected neighborhoods and thus live with powerful insecurity about slipping backward.

We also live with the discrimination that labels us second-class citizens and gnaws at our ability to love each other freely. In a thousand ways—some overtly racist, most subtle and insidious— we are told that being Black is not as good as being White. We remain largely excluded from the ranks of upper corporate management. Taxi drivers let us know our skin is the wrong color when they ignore our hail, then stop at the next corner for a White man. Loan officers make the same statement when they approve mortgages for Whites but not for Blacks earning a comparable salary, or even one that is higher. Our mere presence in certain neighborhoods is enough to trigger a flurry of police reports.

In this environment it is not easy to develop the positive self-image needed to achieve intimacy. The consequences for stable relationships and family life are apparent in the dramatic increase in the numbers of female-headed households. In 1960, after centuries of adversity, 75 percent of Black families still included a husband and wife. In little more than thirty years, those numbers plunged, so that today slightly more than half of all Black children under the age of eighteen live in a home where no father figure is present. Our men are vanishing into prison, falling victim to drugs and alcohol, and dying of AIDS. Violent death is soaring. When the numbers of homosexual men are factored in, the number of eligible Black women to Black men is alarmingly disproportionate.

Some of our people have also fled from family life to avoid humiliation in a society that measures worth by the size of a paycheck. Charles came to see us after he lost his job as a guidance counselor. He was unable to find work in the school districts near his home and eventually took an out-of-state job, commuting home on weekends. Within a few months, he had become romantically involved with a coworker and his emotional and physical distance from his wife and children widened. In therapy, he blamed himself for losing his job, even though budget cuts had actually been to blame, and admitted that he was relieved to escape from the daily pressures of mortgage and child-rearing responsibilities. An affair helped restore his battered ego and made him feel desirable.

At first Charles had difficulty verbalizing his frustrations and could not admit to feelings of failure. We used a process of supportive therapy to help him get more in touch with his own emotions. As he talked, we would point out instances where he was stating thoughts or describing actions, rather than talking about feelings. We also alerted him to body language that was inconsistent with his words—for example, when he said, "I had no choice but to leave town in order to provide for my family," he crossed his arms in front of his body as if to protect himself from a sense of personal inadequacy.

Supportive therapy can be a slow process because it often takes a long time before people are able to be honest rather than defensive, but eventually Charles realized that flight would not restore his sense of worth. His real task was to stop internalizing feelings of failure, to get in touch with the impact of his job loss, and to find ways to share his pain with this wife, rather than excluding her from his emotional reality.

HOPE FOR TOMORROW

Women have coped with the shortage of Black men in many different ways. Some have thrown themselves into careers or the tasks of child rearing, virtually writing off all hope of ever finding a soul mate. Others have stayed in dysfunctional relationships or settled for unsatisfying emotional connections because they are frightened of being alone. There has even been a movement to legitimize "man-sharing" so that every woman has at least part-time access to an eligible companion. A more positive development is the ability of some women to expand their concept of an eligible man. Many Black sisters have discovered that someone who is reliable and has deeply held convictions and a sense of responsibility can make a great partner, even if he doesn't have the world's most well-paying and prestigious job.

We believe the best way to improve the odds that Black men and women can get together in a soul-mate relationship is to bolster the self-esteem of all of our people. Part of the process involves learning how to counteract the demoralizing effects of racism. When Blacks internalize the irrational messages of racism, they feel a sense of worthlessness and powerlessness that creates low self-esteem, depression, and self-defeating behavior.

To combat those feelings, we must change the way we think about racism. Albert Ellis, the psychotherapist who founded rational-emotive therapy, gives us the tools to make that change. Ellis has observed that we are sometimes held back by our own belief systems and uses an A-B-C theory to explain how:

A is the activating event.
B is your beliefs about A.
C is the emotional consequences.

As an example, let us say racial discrimination is the activating event. One man's belief is: "There is no way I can succeed in a society that allows such things to occur." The consequence is that he allows the experience to overwhelm him. By convincing himself nothing can be done, he finds an easy excuse not to try.

Now, let us say another man encounters a racist experience but says, "This is frustrating but I can make an appropriate response." His belief is that the experience says nothing about his worth as a person but shows how ignorant some individuals can be. He then asks, "What can I do to deal with this situation?" The consequence is that instead of dwelling on his powerlessness, he opens himself up to new ways of thinking about a problem. That creates the possibility of planning and executing an appropriate course of action.

The rational-emotive approach is based on the conviction that the way we think about, or perceive, a situation affects how we feel, and therefore how we cope with it. By replacing a faulty belief system with a more positive and assertive one, this approach fosters self-empowerment. It does not completely remove the challenge of responding appropriately to degrading or provocative situations but it does stimulate problem solving and encourages us to take control.

For men, the issues are invariably clouded by pride and a fear of appearing weak. Our clients Harold and Celia had just started to date when they had an ugly confrontation with a White police officer who pulled them over to discuss a relatively minor traffic infraction. Harold bristled at the officer's somewhat condescending tone and hostilities escalated. Celia kept interrupting in an attempt to calm Harold down but that only seemed to make him angrier. The incident ended when Harold threatened the cop and was immediately arrested.

We discussed the dynamics of this dispute in therapy, where Celia expressed shock at Harold's volatility and blamed him for losing it. "I really wonder about getting involved with a man who never thinks about consequences," she said. "Why couldn't you have dealt with the situation more appropriately?" By exploring feelings and answering our questions about motivations, they both realized how embarrassed Harold had been that Celia saw him dominated by a White male. Her intervention only worsened the matter because he did not interpret it as an effort to protect him; instead, he felt betrayed, believing that she was taking the cop's side against him.

An opposite response to a similar situation can also become a source of conflict. After a White clerk had pleasantly served a White customer, he turned to a Black couple named Georgette and Dorin and muttered hostilely, "What do you want?" Georgette was disappointed that Dorin meekly placed his order rather than confronting the obvious rudeness. "It made me wonder whether he is willing to go out on a limb for me," she said.

Whether or not Harold and Dorin responded appropriately to a specific set of circumstances, the psychological and historical roots of their responses are clear. Harold's anger was part of a long struggle among Black men to retain their masculinity despite the battering it takes. Dorin's reaction reflected the hard-learned lesson that Black men can sometimes survive only by swallowing their pride.

In order to change, both men needed to become more conscious of their automatic reactions, which lead predictably to unsatisfactory results. By changing their thought processes and their emotional responses, they learn to address familiar situations in new ways and empower themselves to take more productive and effective actions.

TOWARD AN AFROCENTRIC PERSPECTIVE

The history of Black people in the United States helps explain why Molefi Kete Asante, who chairs the Department of African-American Studies at Temple University in Philadelphia, has nurtured the concept of Afrocentricity. Asante believes that to be whole, Black people must place African values, culture, and history at the center of their very beings. An Afrocentric perspective neither seeks nor expects validation from mainstream White culture. "No longer are we looking whitely through a tunnel lit with the artificial beams of Europe," declares Asante in *Afrocentricity*,[2] a groundbreaking book on the subject. "We have a formidable history, replete with the voice of God, the ancestors, and the prophets. Our manner of dress, behavior, walk, talk, and values are intact and workable when we are Afrocentric."

By contrast, Professor Asante foresees a bleak future for Black people if they do not view their lives from this reference point. "The person's images, symbols, lifestyles and manners are contradictory and thereby destructive to personal and collective growth and development. Unable to call upon the power of ancestors, because one does not know them; without an ideology of heritage, because one does not respect one's own prophets; the person is like an ant trying to move a large piece of garbage only to find that it will not move."

What does Afrocentricity mean to soul-mate relationships? By leaning on the foundation of our African heritage, we hearken back to tribal loyalties and traditional ways of living that allowed the community to endure. These show us that to hurt someone else is to hurt ourselves. To criticize or to strike our partner is an act of aggression turned against ourselves. Our history also reminds us that nurturing, uplifting, and validating a partner are ways to affirm our own best self. Cooperation and interdependency, not competition and self-centeredness—"we" not "I"—become the order of the day.

The expressive, collective African model contrasts sharply with the more individualistic European outlook that views every man for himself, every woman for herself, and each family on its own. Eurocentric societies have historically been paternalistic—the man in charge—and often aggressive and materialistic. When we shackle ourselves to this model, Black folks lose out in two ways. First, we become ever more disconnected from our own rich culture, and second, we become frustrated because racism and social inequalities prevent us from attaining full success as it is defined in White society.

In our view, an Afrocentric approach need not lead us to reject American traditions completely. In *The Psychology of Blacks*, Joseph L. White and Thomas A. Parham describe the benefits of integrating African and American ways. They observe that a life-style emphasizing "individualism, competition, emotional insulation, power, dominance, and control"—that is, the White model—"may achieve success at the cost of being alienated from Black peers and elders who value genuineness, mutual aid and emotional closeness. . . . On the other hand, if the young adult completely ignores the values that will allow progress in the occupational mainstream, he or she will have dramatically reduced the available range of options and the material quality of life associated with these options."[3]

Without turning our backs on the economic opportunities that are part of the American dream, we believe that soul-mate relationships can be structured around the four Afrocentric principles that have been identified by Professor Asante: sacrifice, inspiration, vision, and victory.[4]

Sacrifice. A sense of collective identity allows individuals to give up certain aspects of themselves without regret or resentment in order to advance a larger cause. When a man sacrifices his individual desire so that his partner can get what she wants, when a woman agrees to forgo her own needs to meet those of her soul mate, each one is saying, "Strengthening this partnership means more to me than having my way." To renounce personal desires without expectation of reward is to offer love that comes straight from the heart.

Sacrifice can be an enriching experience, not one that impoverishes, but only when both parties do their fair share. Sometimes the man must say, "I will forgo what I want so that you may have what you want," but on other occasions, those same words must be spoken by his partner. Otherwise, egalitarian relationships give way to exploitation—one person becomes a martyr, enabling the other to assume the mantle of enslaver.

There have been many times in our personal relationship when one of us made sacrifices for the benefit of our relationship. When we first got married, Darlene, who was working on her Ph.D. in a Long Island university close to her parents, made the difficult decision to move to Connecticut. Although Darlene would have preferred to stay in the New York City area, Derek was already well established as a psychologist working at a hospital in Connecticut and both of us were eager to begin sharing our lives. It seemed more practical for Darlene to relocate and she was willing to make that sacrifice so that our marriage could work.

After moving to Connecticut, we discussed whether it would be economically prudent for her to begin job hunting immediately rather than to complete her Ph.D. Derek offered to provide the financial and emotional support necessary for her to obtain the advanced degree, and we have both reaped tremendous professional rewards from that sacrifice.

Sacrifices can take many other forms, of course. A man had carefully saved $1,000 over a period of many months in the hopes of purchasing the mountain bike he had long wanted. However, his wife broached the possibility of buying a computer so that she could supplement the family income by doing some clerical work at home. Although it meant giving up a planned expedition with his brother, he decided that his bike could wait in order to strengthen the family's financial base and help his wife bolster her employment skills.

Another example is rejecting the temptation to begin an affair. Viewed from a "me-focused" perspective, the prospect may sound exciting but it can wound, even destroy, a monogamous relationship. To say no to a budding affair can be seen as an act of self-denial, but it is also a recognition that to damage and disrespect your partner is to damage and disrespect yourself.

Inspiration. An inspiring relationship motivates both partners to stretch beyond their limitations, to aim higher than either one might be able to aim alone. In order to inspire, you must build up rather than tear down; offer encouragement, not ridicule; highlight strengths, not weaknesses. Always, you must tread gently on the feelings of your soul mate; it is never permissible to abuse the power derived from intimacy with ridicule or criticism. In your conversations and your actions, you should be generous with your praise, delicate in your criticisms, and respectful of each other's sensitivities, recognizing that you are both probably carrying with you the baggage of wounds from previous relationships.

The story of a couple who came to us for counseling illustrates the value of inspiration. In the early days of his career, Lester had moved swiftly up the ranks of middle management in a large computer firm. Then the promotions stopped coming—several White men were promoted over him, and after doing a little detective work, Lester found out that no other African-American man in the company had ever risen beyond his current level. He was shocked—he had been raised in an integrated suburban town where he had been protected and this was his first direct experience with the ugly effects of racism.

Soon after this discovery, Lester went into an emotional tailspin that eventually created tension in his marriage. When they came to see us at his wife Debra's urging, Lester was clinically depressed. Through our conversations and Debra's insightful guidance, he was eventually able to realize why he had become so distraught. One of the pillars upon which he had erected his professional life—that he could operate in a color-blind world where skill and hard work would be sufficient to overcome lingering prejudice—had been brutally destroyed. Now he had to rebuild his life with the knowledge that racism, both subtle and virulent, lives on and that he must be proactive in dealing with it.

Debra's support in making the transition was crucial. She had not blamed him when he did not get the expected promotions, nor had she mocked him for his early failure to recognize racism. Instead, she had gently, but persistently, raised the possibility that he was a victim of discrimination. When Lester was finally able to recognize that Debra was right, she stayed by his side to encourage him to explore professional alternatives. Debra's steady, well-paced encouragement, her talk about the importance of risk taking, and her conviction that owning his own firm would empower him, eventually convinced Lester to make the leap that put his career back on track.

Vision. When we bring a shared vision to a relationship, we look beyond our daily struggles toward long-range goals and a better tomorrow. A visionary couple asks, "Where are we going and what steps do we need to take to get there?" Both partners understand the rewards of delayed gratification, set priorities, and chart their future together. An Afrocentric vision is not just about personal gain but about empowering the Black community. As Professor Asante asks, "What is one more diamond ring if there is no sense of destiny?"

Sometimes a vision can also help you move past a quarrel. For example, Louisa and Mark were both furious after a trivial household matter had turned into a nasty quarrel. The couple, who both worked in a teenage counseling center, was not looking forward to the joint workshop they were scheduled to run that afternoon. However, they redirected themselves to the task at hand by saying, "We are upset with each other now, but we have both made a commitment to this youth group and we want to honor it. We must put our differences aside."

By stating their goals, Louisa and Mark were able to give 100 percent to the teens who looked to them for inspiration. It was a fantastic session and everyone got a big high from it. When it was over, they both felt really positive about each other and neither one much cared about the dirty dishes left in the sink. The experience reminded them of their shared vision and allowed them to focus on things that really matter.

Victory. Afrocentric love must also be about victory. "A celebration of ourselves, our aspirations, and our achievements accompanies the victorious aspect of a relationship," writes Asante. "It is a relationship of joy, of power, of peace, of overcoming; it does not speak of failure or losses, of suffering or of oppression."

To be victorious in a relationship means to keep the faith, to think positively, and to know that success is possible and to celebrate it. More than simply a goal, victoriousness is a state of being that acknowledges the strength of our history and the importance of our accomplishments—past, present, and future. In the language of victors, the appropriate phrases are "we can," "we will," and "we must," not "we should try" or "we may not be equipped." As Asante writes: "When the union of man and woman is victorious, nothing can separate you from the love of the people; you are one with each other and, consequently, you are one with the people."

Molefi Asante's principles of sacrifice, inspiration, vision, and victory allow us to tap into the best of our heritage and use it today. Although the long and arduous journey from tribal Africa to twenty-first-century America has yet to bring us to a land of equal opportunity, many Black couples are learning to be intimate, trusting soul mates. It takes extraordinary people to build a constructive relationship upon a foundation of daily struggle against the insult of racism, and yet many succeed. Their lives dispel the myth of an inherent Black pathology and stand as inspiring models for us all.

LEARNING FROM HISTORY

Even a bitter history offers lessons that can help us attain self-knowledge and validate our sense of worth. The more thoroughly we acknowledge the past and understand the myths it has created, the more able we are to transform pain into power that uplifts us.

Below are seven ways to interpret the past so that you can use it to liberate, rather than enslave, your dreams:

Identity: As enslaved persons, we were stripped of our African customs and surnames. In the United States, everything associated with Africa has traditionally been described as evil, mysterious, and frightening.

The myth that lingers: Because my people came here in chains, I feel alienated from both my African homeland and the nation in which I now live. I am not sure who I am.

A *more empowering belief*: I am very proud of my African identity and also claim my rights as an American.

Extended families: The African tradition of extended families was unfamiliar to our European enslavers. They believed the only true families were nuclear families.

The myth that lingers: The extended family structure is deficient and deviates from what is normal. There is something wrong with me because I was raised by my grandparents and because some of the adults who were involved in my upbringing were not blood relatives.

A *more empowering belief*: My extended family provides an enriching source of strength and support for my soul mate and me.

Marriage: Our marriages were outlawed and our ancestors were denied the right to marry. Because long-term commitments were impossible to keep, many of the relationships we formed were temporary.

The myth that lingers: It is okay to sustain several relationships at the same time. I do not have to make a commitment in order to have a partner.

A *more empowering belief*: Until I choose to commit, I can not attain real intimacy. I opt to be faithful in a relationship because having multiple partners will not satisfy me, either physically or emotionally.

Male sexuality: Black men were used as studs to produce the next generation of slave labor. The most valuable men were those who fathered children by many different women.

The myth that lingers: The gauge of my desirability is the number of women I seduce and the offspring I help create.

A *more empowering belief:* I am a valuable human being with much to offer intellectually and emotionally, as well as sexually. Sexual conquests do not define my manhood.

Female sexuality: Slaveowners could summon Black women into their beds at whim; anyone who resisted their sexual advances was punished.

The myth that lingers: I have value only to the extent that I am perceived as sexual. When a man tells me I am desirable, I feel there is a purpose to my life.

A *more empowering belief:* I am attractive because I believe in myself and understand the value of intimacy. Emotionally, sexually, and intellectually, I have much to offer others.

Racism: As slaves, we were not in charge of our own destiny, and to this day, most Black people regularly confront racism, whatever their level of achievement.

The myth that lingers: There are limits to what Black people can accomplish. I am powerless to overcome racism.

A *more empowering belief:* Despite obstacles, I can achieve personal and professional success. I am in control and can find ways to get around roadblocks. My ancestors overcame life-threatening obstacles; surely, I can cope with the lesser troubles I face.

Power and control: Because Black men were often denied educational and economic opportunities, Black women frequently worked outside the home to support the family.

The myth that lingers: If I am a woman, I must be in charge. If I am a man, I am expected to submit passively and am not trusted to make appropriate choices.

A *more empowering belief:* Black men and women can deal with each other as equals while recognizing we are two different human beings. I choose neither to dominate nor to be dominated, but to seek relationships in which power, control, and responsibility are shared.

PART II

▲ ▼ ▲ ▼

LOOKING
INWARD

▲ ▼ ▲ ▼ ▲ ▼ ▲ ▼ ▲ ▼ ▲ ▼ ▲ ▼ ▲ ▼ ▲

CHAPTER THREE

Learning
to Love
Ourselves

▲ ▼ ▲

Despite many heartening examples of Black soul mates, men and women often walk through our office doors to ask for help in finding love or in healing their troubled relationships. Typically, they feel trapped in a complex web of conflict, confusion, mistrust, misdirected anger, and doubt. They don't understand how the web got spun and are at a loss to extricate themselves. They are looking for love but don't realize they must begin the search within themselves.

SELF-RESPECT: FIRST THINGS FIRST

Whether you are single or trapped in an unhappy relationship, you may feel that some perfect person is out there waiting for you, if only you could meet. As a result, you may become driven by the chase—cruising the clubs, pleading with your friends to fix you up, finding yourself too restless to stay home alone, or seeking extramarital affairs. If you don't stay alert, your preoccupation with meeting Mr. or Miss Right may prevent you from asking whether you are truly ready for a long-term commitment.

In order to become someone else's soul mate, you must first be your own. Until you care about yourself, how can you develop a relationship where someone else cares for you? Unless you accept that you are worthy of good treatment, why should anyone else believe it? If you are alone for now, take advantage of your freedom to do some honest soul-searching. By setting aside time for reflection and self-development, you can begin to clarify in your own mind who you are and what you want and need. The more you understand about yourself, and begin to like what you discover, the more prepared you will be to forge a soul-mate relationship.

Many of our clients find it very difficult to feel good about themselves. Children who grew up among adults who constantly criticized them need support in developing the self-esteem that is needed to clear external obstacles. If you were hurt or abused, either emotionally or physically, you may not stop punishing yourself when you grow up. Do you hear your mother saying, "You'll never make anything of yourself"? Did the scorn of your father or the ridicule of a teacher discourage you from setting goals and striving toward a vision? Were you taunted by your peer group? Unless other convincing voices counteracted these early insults, you are likely to have internalized the message that said, "You are worthless."

In a therapy session, Shana described an encounter with her husband, Ross, in which he said, "Playing tennis is a lot more exciting than having sex with you." Shana blamed herself for Ross's lack of interest and tried desperately to win him back. He'd tell her that she was sloppy and fat and she would say meekly, "But I'm trying to change." When Shana sought counseling to discuss her relationship, we asked how she felt about her husband's attacks and she said, "I feel like I should improve." At first, she was unable to articulate pain or express anger.

We worked with Shana to help her develop greater self-respect and ego strength and to understand that it was okay to verbalize feelings. We asked her to consider how she would react if someone treated a friend as Ross had treated her, and Shana admitted that she would be furious. That helped her recognize that she was tolerating unacceptable treatment as a result of a badly tarnished sense of self. Because Ross was unwilling to change, we supported Shana in becoming more assertive. Eventually, she was able to end the relationship and commit herself wholeheartedly to confronting her self-esteem issues.

The exercises we gave her to boost her self-respect are helpful to anyone who lacks confidence. Remember, the goal is to internalize positive feelings, not to use external stimulus, such as buying new possessions, to make yourself feel good.

SELF-ESTEEM EXERCISE: ENJOYING YOURSELF

- Make a list of the things that you like about yourself.
- Do something special to enhance your physical appearance, without spending huge amounts of money—get a new haircut, have your nails done, trim a mustache.
- Find ways to reach out to others in your community.
- Set aside a special time to do the things you enjoy and that make you feel good.
- Join a support group that gives you a place to air feelings and offers a dose of sharing and caring.
- Make an effort to get more exercise—when the body feels good, so will the mind.
- Spend more time with family and friends who have positive attitudes and will nurture you.
- Change your environment—move the furniture around, take a weekend trip, go to a neighborhood you've never seen before, or paint the apartment.

SELF-ESTEEM EXERCISE: CHANGING BEHAVIOR

- Write down the behaviors that make you feel good about yourself. Examples might be spending time with a close friend, doing volunteer work at a day-care center, going to church, meditating, or walking through the park.
- Next, write down the behaviors that leave you with negative feelings, noting what motivates you to engage in these behaviors. Examples of negative behaviors include procrastination, self-denigration, and passivity. Examples of negative motivations include a sense of obligation, external pressures, and lack of confidence.
- Tell yourself you are worthy of engaging in behaviors that leave you with positive feelings.
- Finally, take direct action to stop behaving in self-defeating ways. Write down things you can do to substitute for the negative actions you are now taking. Set aside a period of time every day to engage in self-enhancing behavior. Ask a friend to role-play your new responses to familiar situations.

SELF-ESTEEM EXERCISE: VISUALIZATION

Visualization techniques can also be used very effectively to overcome behaviors you do not like. Consider the path you have been traveling and decide whether it is the right one for you. If not, consider how you might modify it to reflect the direction in which you wish to go. Close your eyes and visualize yourself walking calmly and confidently toward a new set of goals, feeling loved, satisfied, and victorious. Picture yourself deserving love, respect, and kindness.

Here is an example of how you can use visualization: Suppose you are uncomfortable with physical intimacy. Perhaps you flinch when someone you care about approaches to give you a kiss or a hug. Make a conscious effort to imagine a different response.

Visualize someone about to kiss you. Do you automatically pull your shoulders in or cross your hands in front of your chest? Just before you make this reflexive response, say to yourself, "This person cares about me and wants to communicate that in a physical way. I am grateful for the affection. I choose to relax my body and open myself up to messages of caring." Practice this exercise by yourself over and over again so that you react differently the next time a friend makes a physical gesture of affection.

SELF-ESTEEM EXERCISE: LIKING YOUR BODY

Another important dimension of self-esteem involves the way you feel about your body and your physical appearance. The more you learn to accept your looks, the happier, more confident, and more comfortable you will be with yourself and what you present to the world. The first step along the road toward self-acceptance is to really know what you look like. Take a look at yourself in a full-length mirror and describe the different parts of your body. Pay particular attention to skin tone—are you dark, medium, or light? How do you feel about your shade of Blackness? What is the texture of your hair? How full are your lips? Do you feel good about your body size? What messages did you hear about your appearance when you were growing up?

Now make a list of the body parts that please you. Say something positive about each one. If your attention shifts toward body parts you find less appealing, gently return your concentration to those parts you like.

Finally, take a look at the body parts that you do not find attractive. Make statements about each one, such as "My long arms are a part of me and help make me unique and human. God, my creator, has given me these arms and I accept them." Whenever you notice negative thoughts creeping back, be conscious of them and recite that statement again. Try to find something good about each one of your less favorite body parts.

THE IMPACT OF ROLE MODELS

Along with transmitting messages about self-respect, the adults in early childhood provide our most important models for intimate relationships. Consciously or subconsciously, you usually emulate the styles of relating you saw as a child.

If you had the good fortune to grow up around adults who respected and validated each other, you have a head start in becoming a soul mate. Do you recall a moment of crisis when your aunt and uncle stood side by side and gave each other support? A time when your father endured a racial insult and your mother knew just how to comfort him without making him feel ashamed? Perhaps you remember other simple, but symbolic, expressions of love, such as the hot bath your mother drew for your father when he got home after a stressful day, or the steaming hot cup of coffee your grandfather carried into the bedroom for your grandmother when she was barely awake? Because these signs of love were modeled for you, they readily become a part of your own relationships.

If you grew up in a troubled family where there were no positive role models you may have to work harder to sustain close and caring bonds. "I don't even know what I deserve as a Black woman," admitted one of our clients, who has a long history of failed love affairs. "My father sure didn't do much for my mother, and I'm not sure I understand what a good relationship means." In *Black Families in Therapy*,[1] a book targeted at psychologists and counselors, our colleague Nancy Boyd-Franklin offers this insight:

> Many Black people who come for therapy report that they have grown up without experiencing role models for positive male-female relationships. Some have been raised in single-parent homes without a model for this type of interaction. Others have grown up in situations in which they have witnessed angry, hostile, verbal, or physical exchanges as their

only model of male-female interaction. Some Black men and women who have grown up in two-parent, intact families have initially reported a "good" relationship between their parents, but have later admitted that they had only a vague sense of their parents' "couple" interactions. Many older Black couples are very child focused and do not, in fact, have much of a couple relationship.

If you weren't raised by adults who modeled love, trust, understanding, or support, the exercises in this book will be of special value to you as you work toward creating your own example of a positive relationship. We encourage our clients to take heart from people like Joey, whose father abandoned the family when he was young. Joey grew up without seeing a healthy relationship at home, and in his community he witnessed several violent episodes between men and women. As a teenager he was filled with anger, but as a young adult he began to understand that he could learn from these negative experiences; he didn't have to give up all hope for love. With support from friends, Joey began to internalize feelings of self-respect, as well as respect for others, and in time he opened up to the possibility of relating to women in positive ways. He now has a healthy marriage, and his commitment to his family is apparent to all who know him.

One of the techniques that worked for Joey was to surround himself with a network of people who genuinely cared about him. This nurturing network consists of friends with whom an individual can exchange joy, sadness, anger, happiness, excitement, and comfort, and for African-Americans it has been a crucial component of our emotional survival. To make sure that you are surrounded by positive influences, make a list of people with whom you spend significant amounts of time. Then go through the list and ask yourself, "Do I feel valued and appreciated by this person?" If the relationship helps you feel good about yourself, place a plus sign next to the name; otherwise, put a minus sign. Make a conscious effort to surround yourself with the positive people on your list and gradually reduce your contacts with people who don't value or appreciate you.

You can also seek role models by identifying couples whose relationship you admire. Here are some of the clues that alert you to a positive dynamic:

- This couple sets aside time to be alone together.
- This couple demonstrates mutual respect by saying "please" and "thank you" to each other and by complimenting each other in public.
- Both partners appear relaxed together and laugh easily.
- Both partners speak positively to others about their mate.
- Neither partner constantly interrupts the other.
- Neither partner allows others to speak negatively about their mate.
- This couple can disagree in public while making clear that they still respect each other's opinions.

MAKING PEACE WITH YOUR PAST

Making peace with your personal history, and with the people whose influence was not as constructive as it should have been, is one of the great challenges of healthy development. Silencing the whispers you heard as a child that shook your confidence, made you fearful, or raised doubts about your capacity for intimacy and replacing them with positive messages about self-worth are the only ways to liberate yourself. Until you do, you are likely to sabotage one relationship after another.

SELF-ASSESSMENT EXERCISE: THE INFLUENCES OF YOUR PAST

Are you subconsciously imitating behavior you witnessed in your parents or other significant adults, including older siblings, caretakers, or guardians? What lessons were passed along from the adults in your life? Were they conveyed in casual remarks and subtle facial expressions or were the messages overt and repeated often?

Here is an exercise to jog your memory about long-forgotten childhood experiences that may be influencing your ability to find a soul mate today.

Complete the following statements to the best of your ability. Even if you aren't sure of all the answers, provide your best guess. An important part of being ready for a relationship is to be clear about your own past. Thinking about these issues can help you uncover knowledge about your upbringing and the impact that family members have had on you. Once you've begun to deal with these influences and unload the baggage you no longer want, your capacity for a soul-mate relationship will improve.

1. The person in my family I most identified with was _____.
2. I identified strongly with that person because _____.
3. Three significant attitudes about women that person held were _____.
4. Three significant attitudes about men that person held were _____.
5. Three significant attitudes that person held about relationships were _____.
6. When I was fifteen, I swore I would never do these three things in a relationship: _____.
7. I learned most of what I know about the opposite sex from _____.
8. I learned most of what I know about sex from _____.
9. The best thing my parents ever did for each other was _____.
10. The worst thing my parents ever did for each other was _____.

11. Three significant questions about my parents' relationship that I can't answer are _____.
12. I wish I knew these answers because _____.
13. If I had to guess, I'd say that the answers to these three significant questions are _____.
14. The major strength in my parents' love relationship was _____.
15. The major unsolved problem in my parents' love relationship was _____.
16. My family does/does not play an important role in my choice of partners because _____.

Did these questions help you remember some of the significant adult relationships in your life? Did you gain insight about stumbling blocks that trouble you today? Once you understand something more about your past, you might consider opening up a dialogue with your parents or other adults who had an important influence on your development. Talking with them about their relationship, sharing your own joyful and painful memories, and even confronting them about issues that always bothered you can help resolve today's conflicts.

Erasing Old Tapes

If the self-assessment exercise above helped you realize you have internalized some negative messages, it is time to come to grips with your past.

- Listen to the tapes you are playing in your head. What early childhood messages do you hear? Is your father saying, "You are too dumb to succeed in a good job"? Is that your aunt whispering, "You just don't have a bit of common sense. You'll never be able to take care of yourself"? Alana kept hearing her perfectionist father say,

"You should be a lawyer, that's the only way you'll make real money."

- Label the feelings you have when you hear these old tapes. Do they make you angry? Frustrated? Sad? Resentful? How often do you replay the same messages? Alana told us that she heard her father's words constantly and they made her feel chronically anxious.

- Examine the ways in which you have internalized old messages. Because she did not measure up to her father's expectations, Alana constantly berated herself with negative self-statements that said, "I am not good enough. I have not been successful. What I do has no value."

- Recognize that old tapes may be distorted. The adults who recorded the negative messages you hear undoubtedly carried their own psychological baggage. You do not have to take responsibility for their issues. Alana's father drove her hard because he had been thwarted in his own career; Alana had to learn that she was not responsible for his disappointments.

- Understand that you have no control over the past. You cannot change what has already happened and should not allow it to hold you captive; continuing to lick old wounds can become an excuse to stagnate. Rather than saying, "I would be happy now if only my father had been more nurturing to me," Alana needed to acknowledge the past and then move on.

- Take responsibility for yourself in the present. When the old tapes begin playing in your head, push the stop button. Tell yourself, "That is old business. I will no longer repeat these irrational and negative messages."

- Rewind the tape and begin recording positive self-statements. Affirm your strengths by telling yourself, "I am beautiful to myself and to others." "I am sorry if anyone disapproves of me but I do not need their validation to know that I am a wonderful person." "God loves me." "I am worthy of love and will find someone who will love me and treat me well." "I strive to be the best person I can." "I have much to offer a soul mate." Replay those newly recorded messages over and over again in your mind until you really believe them. Instead of telling herself, "I have failed because I did not live up to my father's hopes," Alana was ready to affirm her autonomy. "I am not responsible for pleasing my father. I can pursue what I wish in my own life."

HOW RACIAL IDENTITY IS FORMED

For African-Americans, the task of accommodating the past and building self-esteem is complicated by the challenge of becoming comfortable with your racial identity. That task begins in childhood when your parents first tell you what it means to be Black. If you hear them say such things as "Black people are lazy" or "I'd never go to a Black doctor," it will be a struggle to feel good about who you are and about others.

But if they expressed pride in their heritage and physical appearance, they can help you feel good about yours. One of our clients recalls an orthodontist telling her mother that braces could be used to reduce the size of her daughter's lips. Her mother asked, "Why would I want to do that?" communicating both to her daughter and to the doctor that she considered full lips attractive and desirable, not a source of embarrassment.

The process of defining one's racial identity and striking a healthy balance between African origins and the realities of living in a Eurocentric society evolves slowly. Young adults make very different choices for themselves as they seek a place in society where they feel comfortable and accepted. Some people may choose to minimize or reject their ethnicity. This approach reflects the attempt to identify fully with mainstream society, which seems to symbolize material success and "normalcy," even if it involves turning their backs on their African roots. The danger here is that a young person may become disassociated from the most distinctive aspects of self-identity.

An opposite extreme is to cultivate a totally Afrocentric identity, rejecting White culture completely. We see this in young adults who totally immerse themselves in a Black world, accentuating their roots by the clothes they wear, the cultural activities they attend, the books they read, their circle of friends, and their professional decisions. The reactions of White people, including teachers, employers, and colleagues, may fade in importance. The risk of this approach is that in focusing solely on their Blackness, they lose a sense of common humanity and the ability to relate well to people of other racial and cultural backgrounds.

Most psychologically healthy individuals ultimately find a workable balance between their African and American identities. They become more aware of the realities of racism and the need to appreciate their Blackness without having to put others down. They learn that genuine self-esteem has its origins in unconditional self-acceptance and does not involve condemnation of people from other cultures or criticism of those who have made different choices. They understand how they have been influenced by both African and European cultures, which leads to insights into how they are the same as others, and how they are distinct. Eventually, they may choose to enjoy opera *and* jazz, Judith Krantz *and* Terry McMillan, Steven Spielberg *and* Spike Lee.

This sense of balance also expresses itself in language. Some people "switch up" to relate in the language pattern of mainstream society when they are in certain professional and social circles, then move into Black English with kin. This is perfectly acceptable so long as you are aware of what you are doing and feel comfortable with it. However, switching up should never become a betrayal of self, and you should maintain a clear sense of who you are. Other people maintain the same speech patterns regardless of whether they are talking with Black or White people. The key is to stay conscious of your own identity, to make decisions that allow you to be true to yourself, and to feel good about whatever approach you adopt.

To learn more about how your own racial identity was formed and to develop a greater sense of pride in your heritage, think back to your early experiences with race. Ask yourself some of these questions to understand how your attitudes were formed:

- When did you first became aware of race? Was that experience a positive or negative one? If it was a negative experience, was there a supportive parent, relative, or friend who helped you accept yourself?
- When did you first learn about African-American history? Were you exposed to lessons about African empires and the contributions of Blacks to American society at home, at church, at school, or in the community? Or were you taught only about slavery?
- How important is an African-centered philosophy to you? Are you able to integrate your dual cultural identities?
- Visualize yourself taking a journey through Africa. How do you feel? Are you proud or embarrassed? Do you have a sensation of excitement or one of anxiety? Do you feel close to your ancestors or removed from their experiences?

Once you understand your own outlook better, make a list of things you can do to get more in touch with your racial and cultural background. Examples include increasing your knowledge of the African-American experience by using library resources, attending music or arts events, and celebrating the Black family and community through ceremonial activities, such as Kwanzaa. Seek out friends and family members who are equally interested in cultivating a strong and proud sense of racial identity and make cultural plans together.

A WOMAN'S PLACE

Until we begin to respect our own racial heritage, we impose artificial limitations on who we are, what we can become, and how much we can love each other. Likewise, we must move beyond restrictive stereotypes and unfounded assumptions based on gender bias in order to become true soul mates.

In the 1970s, the feminist movement swept into White middle-class homes to shake up the male-dominated power structure. As their political consciences were born, White women began to define themselves as more than simply wives and mothers. They demanded more visible roles in the workplace and began challenging their partners to share household tasks and to treat them as equals.

Some saw the feminist movement as largely irrelevant to Black families. After all, Black women had never been placed on pedestals; no one ever defined them as fragile ladies who had to be protected. Since the days of slavery, our sisters have been strong and stoic, whatever their pain. After Emancipation, they took the only jobs available to them, generally tasks such as cleaning houses or tending the babies of White women. They were never offered the luxury of staying at home to raise the next generation and were seldom allowed to lay down their burdens, no matter how badly they needed to rest. To this day, whether they are raising their children alone or bolstering their partners' low-wage job with their own income, Black women are rarely in a financial position not to work.

Yet women reared without special privileges need their own brand of liberation. Sojourner Truth, a runaway enslaved person and a spellbinding speaker who never learned to read or write, helped us understand this more than a century ago when she addressed a women's rights convention in Akron, Ohio, with these impassioned words:

> That man . . . says that women need to be helped into carriages, and lifted over ditches and to have the best place everywhere. Nobody ever helps me into carriages, or over mud puddles, or gives me any best place, and ain't I a woman? . . . I have plowed, and planted, and gathered into barns, and no man could head me—and ain't I a woman? I could work as much and eat as much as a man (when I could get it), and bear the lash as well—and ain't I a woman? I have borne thirteen children and seen them most all sold off into slavery, and when I cried out with a mother's grief, none but Jesus heard—and ain't I a woman?

Today, Black women confront forces, both within and outside the Black community, that hold them down not only by virtue of their race but because of their gender. True, we've come a long way since the 1960s, when a militant leader was asked what a woman's position should be in the movement for Black liberation and gave this infamous response: "Prone." Many women are still treated unfairly by their own brothers. "I used to think because Black men have been oppressed by the system they would understand us better," a woman told us during a discussion group. "But many of them just haven't opened their eyes to our issues."

We believe that sexism, like racism, has the potential to put a hammerlock on our lives and eat away at our self-esteem. In our view, there is a place for a distinctly Black version of feminism. Although we approach each other as equal partners in our personal lives, we are sometimes subject to uncomfortable situations in our capacity as professional teammates. On one occasion, we were being honored for our work with Black youth at a local agency and were introduced by the director as "Dr. and Mrs. Hopson." Another time, we were leading a discussion group where one of the participants admonished Darlene for speaking up before Derek. Our critic believed a man should always lead and so perceived Darlene's assertiveness as improper and bordering on disrespect.

We try to deal with sexism in the same way that we confront racism—by staying alert to their subtleties, confronting the issues openly, and rejecting their power to hold us back. To the extent that egalitarianism bolsters the self-worth of all our people and encourages both men and women to nurture and support each other, we are all for it. At its best, it can help women find their place in the world while showing men it is okay to acknowledge emotions and to communicate openly.

However, we understand the fears of those who think feminism might thrust yet another wedge between our people. Where Black women ignore or underestimate the pain experienced by Black men in a White society or direct anger toward those who need compassion, they create tension that is counterproductive to our mutual interests. We need no further excuses for hostility or male bashing, no more weapons that divide us. Black men and women have far more to gain by finding common ground than by allowing resentments or outmoded ideas about gender-defined roles to separate them.

The struggle for genuine liberation sometimes butts against Black men who feel weighed down by racism and need the ego boost that comes from asserting superiority over someone. Cornel West and Bell Hooks see sexism as a tool by which men assert control in the face of oppression. "In North American society, one of the major means by which Black men are empowered is to have power over Black women. For a people who feel already relatively powerless, it becomes a form a competition to not occupy the bottom rung of the ladder. . . . The question is how do we sever Black male notions of empowerment from requiring the active subordination of Black women?"[2] When men and women are able to meet as equal partners, they find ways to answer that question. A confident Black woman learns to distinguish between submitting to boost a man's ego, which is self-denigrating behavior, and offering support, while making it clear that she expects reciprocal behavior from her mate. A confident Black man learns to accept her autonomy and strength and not to see it as a threat to his own.

As you proceed on the journey of self-discovery intended to help you build self-esteem, make peace with your past, and become comfortable with issues of race and gender, you are likely to learn some troubling things. Old wounds may become exposed, and you will often have to confront traits in yourself that you don't much like. At first, you may wonder whether it would be better to leave these topics unexplored, because confronting them can be so difficult. But an injury left to fester cannot heal; it is the courage to admit truth and deal with it that allows you to become whole.

CHAPTER FOUR

The Patterns
of Our
Relationships

▲ ▼

As you begin to understand, accept, and love yourself, you become less likely to participate in a destructive relationship. Until then, you may spin from one failed love affair to another, playing out the same negative patterns each time.

Some women repeatedly become involved with men who physically abuse them. Others may hook up with someone they think they can change, perhaps a man who reminds them of an absent father or someone who expects his needs always to come first. Some men seek out women who will care for them just as their mothers did. Others pair up with partners who try to strip them of their self-esteem with constant criticism and bullying. There are those who walk out on relationships as soon as the issue of a long-term commitment is raised and others who almost beg for intimacy after the first date.

Here are some other examples of abusive statements or behaviors:

• **Put-downs.** Nasty and unproductive criticism such as, "You are so fat, I'm surprised any man looks at you," or, "You are just plain stupid."
• **Being manipulative or disrespectful.** An example is when a man tells you to meet him at a dance and then ignores you the whole evening. Most likely, he will accuse you of paranoia if you confront him.
• **Volatile language.** Yelling, making threats, or cursing in anger is aggressive behavior that should not be tolerated.
• **Sending mixed messages.** The man who first says he wants to break up and then tries to initiate sexual relations is certain to keep you in an emotional tailspin.
• **Being undependable.** Someone who doesn't call as promised, constantly breaks dates, or doesn't show up when he says he will is unlikely to change his pattern anytime soon.

Betty was always getting involved with men who sapped her emotional energy. In therapy, she described an evening in which her current boyfriend, Bernard, arrived at her home in an irritable mood. At first he was cold and uncommunicative, but Betty worked patiently to draw out what was bothering him and he eventually launched into an angry tirade against the "White fools" at work. As Betty cooked and served Bernard dinner, she kept offering him support for his frustrations and encouraging him to complain freely. She never suggested that he might be oversimplifying his problems nor did she mention her own difficult day at the office.

Because Betty told us this was typical of the evenings they spent together, we began to look more deeply at the dynamics of their relationship. It soon became apparent that she often felt obliged to uplift the Black men with whom she became involved. When we looked into her past, we found that her mother had also assumed a caretaking role and subtly conveyed to Betty that she should shower her man with attention to compensate for the wounds inflicted by racism.

Like Betty, many Black women position themselves as Miss Fix-it-alls who believe it is their task to set things right at home. Despite good intentions, Betty did a disservice both to Bernard and to herself. By trying to assume his burdens and offering sympathy instead of encouraging him to take some responsibility for his troubled work environment, she enabled him to remain passive. We call this codependency, a process that occurs when one person enables someone else to maintain dysfunctional patterns of behavior. In therapy, Betty was able to recognize that she was codependent and neglecting her own needs.

SELF-ASSESSMENT EXERCISE: WHERE HAVE YOU BEEN, WHERE ARE YOU GOING?

Identifying destructive patterns is part of the process of shedding the psychological baggage that is preventing you from finding a soul mate. Whether you are involved in a relationship that isn't meeting your needs or looking for that special brother or sister, you can learn more about any difficulty by looking closely at the dynamics of past and present involvements, your likes and dislikes, and your vision of the future. Answer the following questions in detail and then review your answers with a close friend or lover to gain some surprising insights:

1. The five most positive things I have to offer in an intimate relationship are _____.
2. The most honest and loving thing a member of the opposite sex did for me was _____.
3. The most honest and loving thing I ever did for a member of the opposite sex was _____.
4. If I could change one thing about myself, it would be _____.

5. The worst thing I ever did to a member of the opposite sex was _____.
6. The worst thing a member of the opposite sex did to me was _____.
7. My biggest worry is _____.
8. My greatest regret is _____.
9. The major strengths in my current or most recent love relationship are _____.
10. At bedtime, what I usually want most is _____.
11. One secret wish that I have never told to a lover is _____.
12. My most intense longing is _____.
13. Five years from now, I *expect* my love life to have these three significant characteristics: _____.
14. Five years from now, my *ideal* love life would have these three significant characteristics: _____.
15. The main explanation for any differences between the love life I hope for and the love life I expect is: _____.
16. The major unsolved problem in my current or most recent love relationship is _____.
17. The experience of racism has impacted negatively on my relationships in these ways: _____.

Now group your answers together by using them to complete the following sentences. When you have finished, you should have a good overview of what you want and what is standing in the way.

Questions 1, 2 and 3: In my relationship, these are the things I most appreciate: _____.

Questions 4, 5, 6, 7, and 8: In my relationship, these are the things I want to change or stop doing: _____.

Questions 9, 10, 11, 12, 13, 14, and 15: By making these changes, I hope that my relationship will be _____.

Questions 16, 17: By making these changes, I hope that my relationship will no longer be _____.

WHAT NEGATIVE PATTERNS LOOK LIKE

Although everyone searching for love is a unique individual, our counseling experience allows us to pick out some of the patterns that obstruct intimacy. Too many Black men and women are selecting mates based on superficial standards of beauty and attractiveness rather than on the internal characteristics and values that help relationships endure. Do you recognize a bit of yourself in some of the profiles that follow? Don't be alarmed: You have to acknowledge your patterns before you can change them.

The Most Common Mistakes Men Make

"I'll save you." In our practice we sometimes see clients suffering from the "martyr syndrome," a condition that leads men to believe they can restore dignity and joy to downtrodden Black women by assuming their pain. Although their intentions are benevolent, a man who continually champions underdogs generally has his own unresolved psychological issues. For example, a very religious man we counseled became involved with a young prostitute seeking redemption soon after she began attending his church. He told us his goal was to help her become "morally correct," but in therapy, it became apparent that he was acutely uncomfortable with his own sexuality. His real hope was that by rescuing the prostitute, he might also rescue himself.

The drive to assume the burden of someone else's hurt may also be a way of affirming one's own identity and power. In the end, however, "saviors" are doomed to be disappointed—although true soul mates can inspire each other, no man can expect to "fix up" a woman who is not self-aware and ready to change.

"I've got it going on and you'd best do what I say." Young women call them the "pretty boys"—men who know they are attractive and spend a lot of time profiling at the clubs and cruising around the neighborhood flirting with any female around. They thrive on attention but don't feel obliged to return the favor; in fact, they are likely to flee as soon as any demands are made on them. No matter what their age, men who use their good looks to get what they want tend to be socially immature. And why not? With women at their beck and call, they have never had to become self-reliant.

The pretty boys typically want the best of both worlds; although they aren't prepared to take full responsibility for their own lives, they are extremely resistant to anything they perceive as an effort to control them. Often they fly off the handle at any hint of disapproval. Until they learn that a soul mate is not someone who serves their every pleasure and allows them to do anything they please, whenever they want, they won't be ready for a long-term involvement.

"I scored again last night." Some men pride themselves on the number of sexual conquests they make and brag to male companions about them. Even if they are married or involved in a long-term relationship, they view monogamy as a form of surrender. While our history helps explain this behavior, the fact is that a man who plays "musical beds" usually has low self-esteem, feels insecure, and needs the ego boost he gets from having a lot of partners. Keeping score of his sexual accomplishments is a way to convince himself that he is desirable and often suggests there is little else that gives his life much meaning.

"Take it or leave it." Some men exploit the "man shortage" by defining the terms of all their relationships, refusing to compromise or to commit, and offering women no alternatives. Their message is clear: "Either do it my way or I walk." A woman in her early thirties described a scenario with which she has become painfully familiar. "Some guys think it is all about them. Their attitude is, 'I got a good job, I have a nice car, I am marketable, I can have any woman I want. I can have five women. If you don't do this for me, I'll find someone else who will.' " Like the pretty boys, take-it-or-leave-it men rely on their inflated egos and the imbalance of the marketplace to get what they want. The sacrifices involved in a genuine relationship play no part in their lives.

"I look for sparks to fly when I meet a woman." Some men invest a lot more energy pursuing the fantasy of an ideal lover than doing the work to sustain something that endures. Achieving the balance that is part of a healthy Afrocentric relationship is not their goal; if there is romance and sexual passion in the air, they'll stick around, but as soon as a relationship begins to involve struggle, they are gone.

When we talk with men who move through the revolving door of relationships, we try to identify their expectations and sources of discontent. Generally, we find they are operating with illusions—they may tell us, "The magic's gone when the fights begin," or "I'm looking for the electricity that tells me she's the one." Their contacts with women are a series of consecutive fantasies without a reality base upon which to build a more fully satisfying relationship.

"I cannot make it without you." Men who are helpless, insecure, and dependent on women were often raised by overprotective mothers who never emphasized the importance of being self-sufficient. These "mama's boys" tend to latch on greedily to lovers who mother them just as their own parent did. They are passive and childlike, typically making demands and sulking when they don't get their own way. They do not understand the art of assertive communication and avoid direct confrontations for fear of driving away the partner upon whom they rely so heavily. Some even call their wives and girlfriends "Mom" or "Mommy."

"Don't ask questions." Some Black men deliberately maintain distance from the women with whom they become involved. We call them "Ice Men" because they are mysterious about their activities, guarded about their feelings, and extremely reluctant to explore emotional issues. Ice Men feel it is important to be in control, but they are often out of touch with their own underlying needs.

Ice Men were often reared in reserved families that did not express affection openly. Racist as well as other negative experiences may also have shaped their emotional responses. Although physical contact and expressiveness is a traditional part of Black family life, these men may have learned that stifling emotion is a survival tactic. Because they lack models of open warmth, Ice Men also often fear that admitting feelings allows others to exploit them; as a result, they mistake emotional reserve for a sign of strength.

"I am Mr. Independent." Mr. Independent thinks of himself as self-sufficient but he is uncomfortable depending on others for anything. Because he so protective of his autonomy, his partner may feel that she is not valued and that she cannot make a meaningful contribution to his life. Until this man learns that interdependency is at the core of a soul-mate relationship, he may find it difficult to give or receive much from the woman in his life.

The Most Common Mistakes Women Make

"You're in charge." Some women repeatedly become involved with domineering men. Lacking a strong sense of themselves, they confuse control with love and become convinced that men who tell them what to do must really care. This misconception is most likely to flourish among women who had no strong male authority figure in their lives while they were growing up and want to fill the resulting gap by finding someone to protect them. We also see it among women whose male parent was very controlling and left them unable to be assertive with men.

At times, we are all tempted to hand over power to someone else, which spares us the pain of difficult choices and the possibility of making mistakes. Some women feel that allowing Black men to be in charge will help restore their dignity, but we do not believe women should ever give up their own opinions or their sense of personal responsibility. If they do, they send a message that says, "I have so little sense of myself that I am willing to let you take over." That is akin to giving someone carte blanche to exploit you.

"Don't tell me what to do." Some strong Black women who are accustomed to shouldering a lot of responsibility and making their own way have a hard time lowering their guard, even for a man who genuinely wants a balanced and mutually inspiring relationship. Instead, they act tougher than they feel and send signals that say, "Don't get too close" or "I can do everything for myself." They typically have difficulty asking or allowing their partners to nurture and support them.

We applaud outspoken, independent Black sisters who can take care of themselves and refuse to be mistreated—by Black men, White men, or anyone else. But a woman who won't listen to anyone or mistakes compromising for selling out has a lot of learning to do before she is prepared to become someone's soul mate.

"I'll make it up to you." Some women try to smooth the rough road of oppression by showering their men with undue attention. The problem is they go too far—instead of uplifting and inspiring their men, they make excuses for them. That conveys a message that says, "Don't bother, I'll protect you."

A woman who tries to assume the burden of all her partner's sorrows commits two wrongs. By encouraging him to lay all his troubles at her doorstep, she discourages him from becoming self-reliant. At the same time, she allows her own needs for emotional sustenance to be ignored; in a soul-mate relationship, the road toward victory must be walked side by side.

"Your needs always come first." In his writings about Afro-centricity, Molefi Asante warns of the dangers that one person will try to "pimp" off of the sacrifice of another. There is an equal danger that a woman will allow herself to become a servant who puts herself at a man's beck and call. One-sided sacrifice often ends in bitterness, as our client Gloria discovered. When she dropped out of college to put her husband through business school, Gloria accepted an unfulfilling job and abandoned her own dreams. At first, she was content to center her life around her husband, but as he became more successful, she felt increasingly confined and grew resentful. She bemoaned the loss of opportunity in her life but did not know how to say, in essence, "You have been able to achieve so much because we have strived together. Now can we dedicate our energies to some of my work or career goals?"

"I'm waiting for you to mess up." Some Black women have accepted the myth that Black men are lazy. They treat them with an air of condescension and superiority while keeping a firm grip on the household and refusing to share responsibilities. They complain about their heavy load without understanding how they have imposed a burden upon themselves. Women who belittle their men and assume they will do nothing right are unlikely to be surprised; it is human nature to match the expectations that are placed upon us. In the absence of mutual respect, they create a self-perpetuating cycle in which denigration is rewarded by negative behavior, which is followed by more denigration.

"You'd best treat me right." Expensive clothes, fine jewelry, and fancy cars are the key to the heart of this type of woman. A consummate status seeker, this woman does not believe in sacrifice, has a strong sense of entitlement, and feels victorious only when she acquires more expensive toys. There is nothing wrong with having nice things, but she mistakes the amount of cash in a man's pocket with his value as a human being and does not respect men whose priorities are not solely focused on making money. Her outlook is limited. With the wisdom of a few more years, she may alter her shallow outlook, but until then talk about Afrocentric principles will probably fall on deaf ears.

BREAKING OLD HABITS

Once you recognize a destructive relationship pattern in your life, consider its sources and its impact on you. The reason most of us want to break bad habits is that they don't work. They may make you feel unhappy, isolated, or lonely. You may feel trapped or frustrated because you are replaying the same scene over and over again, each time with different partners. Or an awakening may come after four different guys complain that you are too possessive and end their relationships with you. Whatever the impetus, you finally realize you have to change in order to find intimacy.

Where Habits Come From

Looking into your past helps you understand something about the origins of old patterns. Consider some of the family messages and myths you grew up with that are thwarting your capacity for love. By exploring the impact of long-buried experiences and attitudes, you often gain clarity about what is going wrong now.

Margaret can readily identify the origins of her frustrating relationships. She had been raised by a single mother who said to her over and over again: "Don't you sit around waiting for some man to do for you. If you do that, you're going to be waiting forever. You just look out for yourself and make your own way. Black men are always looking for that free ride." When Margaret met a man who genuinely cared about her, her mother's warnings kept echoing in her ears and her actions became a self-fulfilling prophecy. She came to us for help in breaking the cycle of love, suspicion, and dissolution that had characterized past love affairs. Only by stilling her mother's haunting voice would she be able to make the wholehearted commitment she so wanted.

It is also instructive to consider how you might be using current love partners to work out childhood issues. In counseling, it is common to discover that our clients are involved with people very much like one of their parents, which allows them to replay old conflicts and try to resolve them. Sometimes, they take the opposite track, attempting to resolve past conflicts by developing relationships that are dramatically different from those they experienced as children. Either way, the choice is usually a response to unfinished emotional business.

Suppose your woman has that "you'd best treat me right" outlook. Or perhaps you recognize that trait within yourself. First, you'll need to ask: What happened in the past to foster that attitude? Most likely, someone who demands a lot of material possessions was overindulged as a child. If your parents handed out lots of fancy toys to show that you were valued, you may have come to equate being spoiled with being loved. Or the opposite situation may have occurred—as a child you felt deprived and now crave all the possessions you never had. In this way, you hope to fill a void and foster a sense of personal worth.

Another example is the man who is "waiting for sparks to fly." Often, this pattern emerges when the relationships modeled in his childhood were unsatisfactory. Because he had nothing realistic to learn from, he constructs a fantasy of the magic moment

when the ideal soul mate walks into his life and troubles vanish—
and nothing short of that seems good enough.

Clarify Your Goals

To get clear about where you're trying to go, write down your
goals in specific language. You might say, "I want to stop yelling
when I get angry. Instead, I want to be clear about what is
bothering me. I want to say, 'I am angry because . . . ,' " or "I
want to be honest about myself and not exaggerate my educational
achievements. If I am asked about college, I want to say, 'I did
not graduate because I became very involved in political work.'
I want to be accepted for who I am."

The you'd-best-treat-me-right girl might say, "I want to find
nonmaterialistic ways to ask for affection." Instead of angling
for an expensive night on the town, she might decide to think
about simpler pleasures, such as a walk in the park or a night at
home exchanging back massages. The waiting-for-sparks-to-fly
man might say, "I want to stop dreaming about some mythical
electric reaction I expect. Instead, I will make a list of the internal
qualities that matter most to me."

SELF-ESTEEM EXERCISE: CHANGING BEHAVIOR WITH SELF-TALK
It takes awareness and courage to break bad habits and respond
to familiar situations in new ways. When you are ready to approach your relationships differently, you will discover how much
power rests in your hands. We use an exercise called self-talk to
help clients become masters of their mental dialogue and begin
to change familiar habits. Self-talk involves five steps.

• Identify a negative pattern and how it is affecting you. Perhaps
you become anxious when you meet someone new and brag
in order to boost your value in their eyes. Afterward, you berate
yourself by saying, "I must have made a fool of myself with

all my talk. He will never be interested in me now. Why must I be so stupid?"

• Gain control over your thoughts. When you begin to punish yourself for a mistake you have made, put up both your hands and gesture "Stop," while saying the word out loud. Create a private, wordless gesture that conveys the same message for the moments you are in public.

• Forgive yourself and replace your negative thoughts with statements that are reassuring and encouraging. You might say, "It was a mistake to talk so much but it isn't the end of the world. This is not a catastrophe. I can handle this."

• Visualize yourself handling the same situation in a more appropriate way. You might stand in front of a mirror to practice relaxed conversation or put an empty chair in front of you and pretend someone is sitting there. Or find a friend who will help you role-play the conversation you wish you'd had.

• Try again. If you have a chance to meet the same person, you might say: "Hi. Last time we met I was so nervous that I kept rambling on about myself. I'd like to learn more about you." If that opportunity doesn't present itself, get ready to use your practiced dialogue next time you meet someone new.

SELF-ESTEEM EXERCISE: LISTENING TO YOUR INNER VOICE

Another way to guide yourself away from negative patterns and toward your true essence is to listen closely to the self-enhancing voice that lies within. As you learn to respect and to love yourself, your inner voice becomes a spiritual force that helps you confront the challenges of everyday life with a positive attitude and make the right decisions. Take these steps to cultivate a voice that sends positive and insightful messages:

• Set aside at least fifteen minutes a day to sit quietly by yourself.

- Take time to appreciate your senses. What do you smell in your environment? Do you like the scent of your own body? Can you catch a subtle aroma of flowers in the air? Look in the mirror. Do you like what you see? Stroke your arm, legs, and face. How does that feel? Listen to the sounds around you. Do you hear nature's music? What does your inner voice say about what you smell, see, touch, taste, and hear?
- If you are faced with a big decision, focus on how the alternatives affect your senses. What is your inner voice saying about the choices before you? Make a list of your sensory responses to each option. Do you feel hot or cold when you think about a certain choice? Does your body tense or relax? Do loud internal voices warn you against a certain course? Does it smell right? Is there a sweet taste associated with your decision?
- As you begin to understand and accept the wisdom of your inner voice, allow it to become your guide. Trust in yourself as a spiritual being, aware of the world around you, open to change, and able to grow. Refuse to become bogged down by negative patterns. Realize that you are an attentive and sentient human being traveling on the path toward your true self.

WHEN VIOLENCE ENTERS THE PICTURE

Many of the negative patterns we've described in this chapter leave emotional scars, but occasionally abusive behavior escalates into physical or emotional violence and leaves an even uglier mark. The origins of violent behavior may be rooted in abuse that was inflicted in childhood, the absence of adults to model effective ways of dealing with conflict, or the frustrations, rage, and disappointments that accumulate in a racist society. Some

Black men who were raised by single mothers may have been the target of displaced anger directed at their absent fathers and learned that aggressive behavior is an appropriate way to deal with conflict and disappointment.

Violent men are often themselves victims of violence. That knowledge weighed heavily in our minds when we were asked to evaluate a troubled five-year-old boy named Aaron. Aaron, who had been repeatedly beaten by his mother's boyfriend and witnessed her being abused, was referred to us after he began to punch girls in his class and to strike his female teacher. After looking carefully at his family history, we painfully recommended that he be removed from his present home and placed with a relative in the hopes of breaking the vicious cycle in which an abused child grows into an abusive adult. Aaron's only hope, we believed, was to be raised in an environment where he would learn it was not normal behavior for people to harm each other.

A violent man is often asserting control in the only way he knows how—by demonstrating superior physical strength. But his behavior actually reveals the extent of his powerlessness. "Some men, unable to contain the emotional storms, struck out at those who would be least likely to destroy them," wrote Martin Luther King. "They beat their wives and their children in order to protest a social injustice, and the tragedy was that none of them understood why the violence exploded."[1]

Women who accept abuse from men, be it physical or emotional, invariably carry their own unresolved conflicts into a relationship. Low self-esteem is often at the root of the trouble—some women do not value themselves enough to believe they deserve better treatment. In some cases, they long for the strong man who was absent in their own childhood or feel too uncertain of themselves and their place in the world to assert their rights. Or they confuse abuse with genuine love, telling themselves: "He wouldn't treat me this way if he didn't really care," or, "He loves me and he is doing this for my own good." A woman may also collude with an angry Black man because she feels guilty about her own privileges—her unspoken message is, "He has a right to his rage and I must allow him to vent it on me." Women who have been physically or sexually abused as children are especially vulnerable to abusive relationships in adulthood.

Whatever its psychological underpinnings, abuse is a devastating symbol of failed communication and can destroy a relationship. Neither physical nor emotional violence should ever be tolerated. Accepting destructive behavior or making excuses for it is a form of collusion that enables your partner to evade responsibility. If you are involved with someone who is threatening you or causing you pain, you need to remove yourself from the relationship until that person commits to getting professional help, follows through, and begins to make genuine changes.

Cali had moved out of her house after arguments with Brad about unpaid bills and child-care responsibilities turned increasingly violent. She told him she would be willing to participate in counseling to improve their communication and to break the cycle of violence but she also said: "I will not tolerate your abuse. I am worthy of better treatment."

By refusing to collude in her own punishment, Cali asserted her power. As we helped the couple become aware of their issues, they realized this was a watershed event. Brad had always dominated household decision making, and Cali, who had grown up in a permissive home with a father who set no limits for her, had at first been happy to have a man in charge. As Brad demanded more and more control, and finally struck Cali in an effort to win obedience, she realized their relationship was out of control.

By taking time out, Cali recognized that her longing for a stereotypical father figure had left her open to abuse. Brad, for his part, recognized that his insistence on being in control was a way to vent his frustrations about his job, where he felt powerless. Because they were both willing to explore their issues and make changes, Cali and Brad could salvage their marriage.

This is not always possible. If a relationship is causing you harm, you and your partner may have to part if you cannot break the destructive pattern. Xanda's boyfriend never actually laid a hand on her but found many opportunities to abuse her emotionally and to diminish her self-esteem. For example, he constantly mocked her efforts to return to school for a graduate degree. Initially, Xanda had accepted his judgments of her, thinking to herself, "Pat doesn't think I'm smart enough to go back to school. He must be right."

After months of therapy, she began to recognize that no one had the right to treat her so shabbily. When Pat kept rebuffing her efforts to confront their issues, Xanda broke off the relationship. Free from his negative messages, she enrolled in school and thrived as she began to cultivate neglected talents.

Xanda's breakthrough is a paradigm for all African-Americans. She blossomed by learning to affirm her own self-worth and to reject abuse. After discovering the destructive power of negative messages, she began working with positive self-statements. Over and over again she told herself, "I am good at many things. I am a valuable human being with a lot to offer others. I do not need to settle for less than I deserve." Slowly, she came to believe her own words and found that men responded to her confidence. She was then ready to be a true soul mate.

LOOKING FOR LOVE IF YOU ARE SINGLE

After you have armed yourself with self-knowledge and self-respect, how do you go about finding someone who will appreciate your value and treat you well? It helps to be patient and to fill your life with activities you enjoy. Don't put everything on hold until a soul mate comes around.

But do make an effort to get to appropriate settings—places where you'll have a good time even if you don't meet a promising partner. Consider the source when you're looking to meet someone new; if you want a churchgoing man, you're unlikely to find him in a nightclub. Instead, go where the chances are good that you will find someone who shares your values. Spiritual centers, Black professional associations, community organizations, college fraternities and sororities, and introductions from friends are all alternatives to pursue.

Then, just try to be yourself. When men and women get together to talk about the issues that interfere with intimacy, they always say it is hard to break the ice with strangers. Some men complain that women are hostile to their most casual advances. Said one, "I introduce myself to someone and her first reaction is, 'Hello, my name is Sue and you can't have none.' " Women have their grievances too. They complain that most men care too much about appearances—expecting to see them in tight dresses or expensive clothing and decked out with gobs of makeup, fancy hairdos, and manicures—and not enough about their inner selves.

Sometimes, single people unintentionally distance themselves from others, even when they are eager for intimacy, because they are fearful of being hurt, rejected, or mistreated. They may say to themselves, "I hope I can meet a nice guy and talk to him tonight," but their speech and body language convey an attitude of hostility that puts people off. If you recognize a gap between what you want and how you behave, you have to work to change your habitual approach. Practice some of the self-esteem exercises in this chapter and the previous one.

For example, imagine a good-looking man headed your way. Think about your usual reaction: Do you turn away from him before he has said a word? Do you send a signal that asks, "What do you want from me?" Do you roll your eyes because you don't trust what he will say?

Consider how you might handle a meeting in a more welcoming way. Say to yourself: "I want to be warm when a stranger greets me because he may turn out to be an interesting person." "I would like to be open to new encounters." "I want to stop being hostile toward a man when I meet him. Instead, I want to smile and engage in pleasant conversation."

Work at being friendly, approachable, and nonjudgmental. No one likes being rejected, so if you're interested, let it show. Let a brother know when he has caught your eye. Find ways to tell that special lady you are interested without coming on too strong. If you become aware that your body language is tense or overprotective, practice more relaxed postures in front of the mirror. Think about good topics for casual dialogue and role-play them with a friend. Who knows? You just might find yourself stepping onto the path that is headed toward victorious soul-mate love.

Here are some hints for letting others know you are open to a conversation:

- Make eye contact and smile at people around you.
- Introduce yourself to a stranger.
- Be an attentive listener. Paraphrase the words being spoken to you and make supportive comments about them.
- Use body language to convey interest. Stand or sit comfortably and position yourself reasonably close to the person with whom you are speaking.
- Ask about the other person's interests and describe your own. Look for common ground and emphasize it.
- Remember that humor is a great tool for putting people at ease. There's nothing like shared laughter to bring you close.
- Be generous, but sincere, with compliments. People like to be told they are wearing a nice outfit or have a nice manner and a pleasant speaking voice.

- If you feel comfortable with someone, touch them casually. You might brush a piece of lint off a man's shirt or gently touch his hand while you are talking. Stay alert to signals that tell you whether the person is receptive to physical contact.
- Take a slow, deep breath, exhale gently and relax. Focus on enjoying your personal and social connections.

PART III

▲ ▼ ▲ ▼

THE TOOLS FOR MAKING IT WORK

▲ ▼ ▲ ▼ ▲ ▼ ▲ ▼ ▲ ▼ ▲ ▼ ▲ ▼ ▲ ▼ ▲ ▼

C H A P T E R   F I V E

Twelve Lessons for Developing Intimacy

▲ ▼

Now that you understand a little bit more about yourself, you are better prepared to tackle the challenges of developing genuine intimacy. To accomplish that mission means shedding certain fantasies. It would be wonderful, for instance, if someone always knew what we wanted, without our ever having to say a word about it. It would be convenient if we could always have things our own way. But in lasting relationships, these are mythical ideas that hold us back; to move ahead, we need to deal with reality.

Before introducing the twelve lessons of intimacy, let's take a quick look at the truths we must substitute for myths in order to sustain a soul-mate relationship:

The myth that impedes me: If you really loved me you would understand what I need.

The reality that moves me forward: My partner is not a mind reader. I must learn to verbalize my needs.

The myth that impedes me: I know exactly how I want my soul mate to look and act. If someone does not fit the profile I have in my head, I will not allow any kind of relationship to grow.

The reality that moves me forward: I cannot expect my partner to squeeze into a box that I have already designed. I must learn to love him as he is, not as I would like him to be.

The myth that impedes me: When I finally meet the right partner, my troubles will be over.

The reality that moves me forward: Another person cannot make me whole. I must look inward to derive the sense of self-worth that will prepare me for a soul-mate relationship.

The myth that impedes me: In a genuine soul-mate relationship, there are fireworks and passion all the time.

The reality that moves me forward: I must work on maintaining and building emotional and physical intimacy as well as romance.

The myth that impedes me: I can change my partner to make him better.

The reality that moves me forward: I accept my partner as he is. My role as a soul mate is to motivate, encourage, and inspire, not to make demands.

The myth that impedes me: If this relationship does not work out, it will be an emotional disaster for me.

The reality that moves me forward: I can handle disappointments in a relationship. It does not mean that I have failed or that I will never find true happiness with someone else.

LESSON ONE: COMMITMENT IS A DECISION

In the early stages of a relationship, both parties may be dating other people, but as things become more serious the subject of exclusive commitment is likely to arise. Are you ready to assume the responsibility that entails? Often the answer to that question is not a simple yes or no. Commitment involves sacrifice and long-term planning, and some couples who say they are ready to make a commitment—and may honestly believe that they are— actually end up sabotaging their love.

A client of ours named Ann came into therapy complaining that she wanted to settle down and have children but that two recent relationships had fallen apart. As we worked with Ann, it became clear that she was finding ways to shatter any bond that became too close. She clung too hard to one man until he broke off the relationship, telling her that he felt strangled. Then, after provoking a major confrontation with another man, she declared she could not stay with someone who yelled at her. Eventually, we traced Ann's conflicts back to her childhood, when she had been sexually abused by an uncle who helped raise her. The result was a pathological fear of trusting men. While fear was an appropriate response to the trauma, it developed into pathology when it was displaced and generalized, impairing her ability to function.

Although Ann thought she wanted to be married, she was ensuring the opposite outcome by cutting off ties as soon as they became intimate. She now recognizes she has a lot more work to do on herself before she is truly ready to make a commitment.

It is important not to insist on rushing commitment. Setting deadlines, such as wanting to be married by a certain age, only imposes artificial pressures and may interfere with sound decision making. The time to make a commitment is when both parties feel confident about it and are ready to share their vision of the future.

Steve and Ruth began talking about an exclusive commitment after they had been together for about six months. "If we are going to strive for closeness, it is important to me that we be

monogamous," Ruth told Steve. "The sort of intimacy I'm looking for can't happen if there's no long-term commitment." Steve
initially had some anxiety about making promises. He had been
involved in a relationship that ended painfully the year before
and felt the need to move slowly on this one. "I respect your
needs but I'm not ready to commit to a lifetime together," he
said.

Because they verbalized feelings openly and without hostility,
neither Ruth nor Steve interpreted each other's statements as an
ultimatum. They compromised by agreeing not to date other
people but to spend some weekends apart to give Steve the space
he needed. A year later, they were still together and moving slowly
toward a more fully committed relationship.

Myth has it that commitment is more important to women
than men, but in our practice we have discovered this issue is
more complicated and less predictable. Some of our male clients
are very eager to have a committed relationship while some of
the women we counsel are quite ambivalent about it. The reasons
are varied. Some women may worry about the impact of commitment on their careers or fear that controlling men will expect
them to set aside their own pursuits. Others have been warned
from an early age that Black men are unreliable and may not be
able to shake themselves free of that negative message.

Whatever their reasons, many women approach a new relationship convinced it will not last. In therapy clients tell us, "I recognize that this man may not always be there for me and I need
to be able to take care of myself." Although we believe that women
need to be self-reliant and should feel good about themselves even
without a man in their lives, we are concerned about this assumption of failure. Too often it can discourage constructive struggle
and become a self-fulfilling prophecy. We try instead to help our
clients find a middle ground, supporting their efforts to be independent while modeling a relationship that allows them to com-

mit to each other without shedding their individual identities.
These are some of the fundamental principles of commitment:

Commitment is seeking ways to enhance the relationship.

Commitment is thinking about your partner and not just
about yourself.

Commitment is being faithful.

Commitment is being loyal and responsive.

Commitment is being dedicated to maintaining the relationship.

Commitment is focusing on your partner's needs as well as
your own.

Commitment is being sensitive to your partner's past hurts
and helping in the healing process.

Commitment is visualizing yourself in a long-term relationship with your current partner.

Commitment is working to overcome barriers to communication.

Commitment is hanging on during hard times.

Commitment is planning for the future and establishing
goals together.

LESSON TWO: WITHOUT TRUST, THERE CAN BE NO VICTORY

Trust is an essential ingredient of a soul-mate relationship. We
learn our first lessons about trust as infants and children when
the adults upon whom we depend completely demonstrate that
they will meet our needs consistently. If childhood experiences
have encouraged us to trust others, we learn to be honest about
our feelings, confident that we will be neither mocked nor exploited. We share our inner selves, knowing that other people
will respect our vulnerabilities, safeguard our confidences, and

respond appropriately to our concerns. The more we trust, and are rewarded with intimacy, the more emotionally able we are to open ourselves up to others.

By contrast, if experience has given us reason to distrust others, achieving intimacy becomes much harder. A human being who feels his or her trust has been violated or expoited often becomes more cautious and self-protective. Whether we have been wounded by our families, our love partners, or the society around us, many Black people have had painful experiences that cause them to disguise their true selves from other people.

An intimate relationship is a source of joy only when you have full faith in your partner's loyalty and long-term dependability. Psychologists White and Parham remind us that trusting others involves both internal and external processes. First, you must trust yourself enough to take a risk on someone else, and second, you must have the skills to assess relationships appropriately.

How do you know whether your partner is trustworthy? In the early stages of a relationship, you may have to tolerate some uncertainty and risk. If the person you are dating is sending consistent and positive messages that say "I am trustworthy," only a leap of faith will allow you to know for sure. By assuming the best, rather than waiting for the worst, you can help perpetuate a cycle of candor, deepening trust, commitment, and more candor. If you cannot do this, a wall of doubt may rise that eventually becomes impossible to scale.

Here is an exercise designed to help you judge a potential mate's trustworthiness. Answer the following questions with *never, rarely, often, or always*:

1. I know that I can depend on you to support me under any circumstance.
2. Your behavior is erratic and I never know what to expect from you.
3. I fear that we will grow apart.

4. Although I am unsure of the future, I have faith that we will be together.
5. I cannot rely on you to get anyplace on time.
6. You keep your promises, even when that is a difficult thing to do.
7. When you are under stress, you lash out at me.
8. I am certain that you are sexually faithful.
9. I know that it is safe to come to you with my concerns when I feel vulnerable.
10. You are threatened when people disagree with you.
11. You respect my point of view even when you see things differently.
12. You have difficulty admitting your mistakes.
13. When you give me your word, I am confident it is true.
14. You gossip about or criticize other people.

Scoring: For questions 1, 4, 6, 8, 9, 11, 12, and 13, score: *always*—4 points; *often*—3 points; *rarely*—2 points; *never*—1 point.

For questions 2, 3, 5, 7, 10, and 14, score: *always*—1 point; *often*—2 points; *rarely*—3 points; *never*—4 points.

Add up your points. The optimal score is 56 but anything over 45 provides a clear indication that you are involved with a trust-worthy partner. The lowest possible score is 14 but anything below 25 is probably cause for grave concern: There is little or no reason to trust this person and you cannot expect to build a soul-mate relationship on such a shaky foundation.

Exercise caution with partners whose scores fall in the middle of the spectrum. There is considerable uncertainty as to whether they will rise to the level of your trust.

Even if your partner earns a high score, it takes confidence to expose yourself to the possibility of getting hurt. Fortunately, the payoff can be substantial. By deciding to trust someone, you set the stage for openness and make it clear that you expect honesty and loyalty in return. When they respond, you know you have found a soul mate who will talk to you about issues of concern in nonthreatening ways, accept you as you are, without undue criticism, and stand by your side, no matter what the circumstances.

LESSON THREE: COMPROMISE IS NOT A DIRTY WORD

In one of our discussion groups, an articulate Black woman writer said, "I think good relationships are worthwhile but I don't think compromised relationships are worth anything at all." We have given a lot of thought to her remark because it highlights an important distinction: Soul mates *do* compromise but they *don't* sell out, violate personal principles, or settle for less than either one of them deserves.

Perhaps you, like many of our clients, have an initially negative reaction to the thought of making compromises. You may be fearful or anxious about having to give up something that is very important or reluctant to do anything that makes you appear malleable. People who have been mistreated or exploited as children find it especially difficult to compromise because of deep-seated fears that someone will try to take advantage of them. Whatever the reason, clinging stubbornly to what you want, instead of struggling to reach consensus, can turn a relationship into a never-ending power struggle.

It requires self-confidence and a foundation of trust to reach satisfactory compromises. In a soul-mate relationship compromise is not one-sided and does not leave either partner dejected about losing a battle. Instead, it allows you to feel victorious about resolving a disagreement on terms that feel comfortable. In couples counseling, we help clients identify possible compromises by encouraging them to consider what they really need, and then what they may be willing to give up to get it. It is a two-step process:

Step one. Define your fantasies. How would you like this issue to be resolved if you could have things your way?

Step two. Where are you willing to make concessions? What is too important to you to negotiate?

Once the parameters of the discussion have been clearly established, it becomes easier to move closer together until you reach common ground. Often the compromises that nurture a relationship are relatively minor. One man we know had no family tradition of celebrating birthdays but his wife loved to get flowers, gifts, and special treatment on that day. "I make a big deal of her birthday because it is important to her," he told us. "If someone matters in my life, I'm going to find out what she likes and give it to her even if it means changing my own habits." We believe that if all our brothers and sisters could be so accommodating, we would see far fewer conflicts and a lot more love.

LESSON FOUR: TARGET YOUR ANGER WHERE IT BELONGS

When conflict arises, one of the first questions a self-aware couple should ask is: What is really bothering us? Sometimes, the source of the problem is not immediately apparent. For example, instead of responding directly to a racist insult, we may lay our frustrations at the doorstep of someone we cherish. This was apparent with Candice, a social worker who counsels emotionally disturbed adults in a psychiatric unit. Candice had been attacked by one of her patients. Along with the injuries she sustained, the experience left her traumatized and disappointed in the White coworkers who had not moved quickly to assist her.

Weeks later, after she and her husband had given a dinner

party for a dozen friends, Candice exploded. The provocation seemed minor—Candice was cleaning up in the kitchen while her husband, Lawrence, talked with a friend in the living room. Suddenly, she burst into the room in tears and accused Lawrence of "never doing anything to help," adding that she felt she couldn't trust him anymore. In therapy, we explored the intensity of her reaction and helped her see how she was displacing her feelings of abandonment at work onto Lawrence. In effect, she was saying to him, "Other people I trusted didn't come through for me when I needed them and I'm not sure you will either." Once she understood the real source of her anger, Candice was able to focus on expressing it more appropriately. Lawrence, for his part, recognized that after her traumatic experience Candice needed some extra support.

LESSON FIVE: KEEP YOUR BALANCE

In a healthy soul-mate relationship, your roles as friends, partners, and lovers are balanced. Because you are friends, both of you are dependable and supportive, in good times and in bad. The channels of communication are always kept clear. As partners you work together on common goals, complementing each other's skills and apportioning responsibility and credit fairly. And as lovers you share intimacy in whatever way you choose— whether it is a candlelight dinner in a hideaway restaurant, a romantic greeting card, or exploring new ways to heighten sexual pleasure—so that the flames of passion are never allowed to cool.

The challenge in any relationship is to be sure that each one of these roles gets its fair share of attention. Too many couples communicate only enough to get the bills paid or to make child-care arrangements, forgetting to take time out for romance. Others are sexually passionate but don't share common interests outside the bedroom and seldom go out together.

One evening at a dinner party, a couple named Marvin and

Shana shared an insightful story with us. As hospital adminis-
trators who are deeply involved with their work, they relish their
professional compatibilities and regularly share stories, talk about
health policy, and bounce ideas off each other. However, they
find it a constant struggle to keep the partnership dimension of
their relationship from becoming too dominant. One Saturday
morning, they had barely opened their eyes when Marvin mentioned an interesting article he had read in the latest issue of a
scientific journal. Shana was about to comment on it when the
absurdity of the situation suddenly struck them both. Here it was
the weekend, the day had not even gotten started, and they had
already plunged into a heavy conversation about hospital
management.

Marvin and Shana admitted that the incident brought home
the fact that their intellectual lives were receiving more than a
fair share of nourishment. Fortunately, they were able to laugh
about it and have since worked consciously to create a better
balance in their relationship. It is still a struggle, they say, but
at least they are both more aware of the pitfalls and are trying
harder to avoid them.

LESSON SIX: SHED THE ATTITUDE OF HELPLESSNESS

Because of the insidious ways in which racism limits the options
of African-American people, it is easy to become discouraged.
When people are convinced they cannot succeed, no matter how
hard they work and regardless of what they do, they usually stop
trying. Even minor obstacles become overwhelming. They no
longer feel in control of their destiny and accept defeat. This
passive condition is called *learned helplessness*.

Our history shows we are strong enough to overcome passivity
if we expect the best from each other and from ourselves. By
replacing the negative tapes we play in our heads with affirmative

messages, we begin to reclaim our power and move closer to realizing our vision. When you encounter a problem at work, don't assume "I'm not going to be able to do this, I don't have the skills." Instead, remind yourself "I'm a diligent worker dedicated to this project and I'm going to find a way to get it done." When you face a new challenge, stop saying, "I can't," and begin saying, "I'll do my best" or "If I don't know something, I'll do what is necessary to learn it."

This sort of affirmation is also the best vehicle for achieving intimacy. When you encounter problems, don't conclude, "This relationship is doomed." Invest in yourself and your soul mate with messages that say, "I'm really committed and I know we'll be able to work through this." It is also important that you allow each other the space to make your own decisions and your own mistakes. When men or women assume full responsibility for their partner's life, they teach them to be helpless. When they inspire each other instead, pride and the spirit of "I can" and "we can" are fostered.

LESSON SEVEN: OUR SISTERS ARE NOT BITCHES

One of the uglier words we hear our brothers use to describe their sisters is "bitch." Whether they have picked up the insult in childhood or are still hearing it from friends today, many men are unable to look beyond the pervasive stereotype that portrays Black women as hard-edged and controlling. "There is no pleasing those bitches," one client said to us.

Recently, we asked a group of men exactly what they mean when they say, "That sister is a real bitch."

"A woman who is uncompromising, someone who always has to have things her way," said one man.

"Someone who is vindictive," suggested another speaker.

"To me, it is someone who comes off with an unpleasant

attitude," explained a third. "Say I meet a woman and say to her, 'How are you doing? You are looking nice today.' If she just rolls her eyes with an air of nastiness or says something like, 'Oh please,' that's being a bitch. A woman who doesn't want to be bothered should learn just to say so."

For some people, the word has become so commonplace it is not always even intended as an insult. "I'm going out with a fine-looking bitch tonight," a man might say. But even if it is not intended to be denigrating, the word has no place in our vocabulary. If Black folks are going to stop battering each other and begin addressing each other with more respect, we must recognize that language has an impact. We enjoyed the story told to us by a young filmmaker who ran seminars to boost the self-esteem of teenagers. He opens each session by asking all the girls to rise and then says to the seated boys: "These are not bitches. They are our sisters. If we are going to talk about taking care of each other, let's start by agreeing on that right now."

LESSON EIGHT: OUR BROTHERS ARE NOT DOGS

As children many of us heard our own mothers describe Black men as oversexed, aggressive, lazy, or directionless. Today some of our folks say the same things. How often have we heard words like those spoken in anger by a single mother struggling to raise two children on a secretary's income—"Black men just aren't any good. All the brothers are dogs"?

Notice that she does not say, "I've had a hard time with my man," or "Some men aren't mature enough to accept responsibility." Rather, with one derisive phrase, she dismisses every last African-American male, some ten million over the age of fifteen by the last census count. The result of this man bashing is to increase our sense of alienation from each other and to foster distrust. We wince when we hear our sisters dismiss Black men with so little respect because it suggests they have given up the hope of having meaningful relationships. At a women's group we recently asked the participants to tell us what they mean by the word "dogs," and they had quite a few derogatory things to say.

"It is a guy who won't commit. He just sleeps around and comes off with an attitude that says, 'Your feelings don't matter to me. You should be happy enough just to have a man in your life.' "

"Someone who is insincere, maybe someone who'll lie to get what he wants. He's completely out of touch with his own feelings and you can't talk with him about things that really matter."

"It's one of the 'good-time men' who give a woman a line to get her into bed but don't care about developing a relationship. Or maybe he'll develop a relationship and still have sex with other people without any sense of remorse or betrayal."

Our sisters don't automatically intend to be denigrating when they call men dogs. The word has become so commonplace that in some circles it has come to mean "boys will be boys." But it is nonetheless time to change our vocabulary: Our men are not dogs, they are our brothers.

LESSON NINE: SOUL MATES CANNOT MAKE US WHOLE OR BE OUR MIRROR IMAGE

In our struggle to become whole—to recover from deficiencies in our upbringing, to counteract weaknesses we perceive in our character, or to find ways to attain our vision—we often select soul mates who have characteristics that we are missing or believe we are. This is partly explained by an intriguing psychological concept we call *compensation*.

Hugh, for example, is intense about everything he does—he trains for marathons, works twelve-hour days, thrives on pressure, and feels fine after only a few hours of sleep. He was drawn to

Mandy's placid manner—she was contented, valued unscheduled time and spontaneity, and set an example that calmed him down. Ironically, the very traits that initially attract two people to each other later become the biggest source of their conflicts. Hugh was soon prodding Mandy to "do more with your life." Mandy, who at first had been charged by Hugh's energy, kept telling him to "chill."

Their relationship illustrates the absurdity of trying to convince our partners to become more like us, an approach that only leads to frustration. We dare our clients to break this pattern by taking risks and doing things differently. The first step is to remember the attributes that drew you together. Then, instead of trying to overhaul each other's personalities, we emphasize incremental changes that allow you both to maintain your distinctive personalities while finding common ground.

LESSON TEN: BELIEVE IN THE POSSIBILITY OF CHANGE

Many couples do not realize it is possible to make meaningful changes in a relationship; they believe their choice is to accept existing problems or to split apart. In most cases, patterns of relating become so entrenched that the two parties no longer listen to each other. Instead, they rehash the same argument over and over again, sometimes for years.

In our counseling practice we emphasize that relationships can be improved if both parties are willing to do the work. By modeling our own methods of communication and conflict resolution, we challenge couples to take the chance of approaching each other in new ways.

Sharon and Tyrone came into therapy to deal with her feelings that he was cold to her. Although they had a "fairly good" relationship, Sharon longed for small signs of Tyrone's affection—hand-holding, a quick kiss in public, an unexpected hug. Tyrone said that his family had always been very reserved and casual physical contact did not come readily to him. We suggested he try greeting Sharon with a kiss every evening when he came home from work, even if he felt a little uncomfortable doing so.

Tyrone was eager to cooperate, but Sharon's response on his first attempt was to say, "You are doing this mechanically because I've asked you for it." This puts Tyrone in a no-win position and leads to a dead end. We urged Sharon to recognize the sincerity of Tyrone's effort and to understand that criticizing his efforts or labeling them as less than genuine was counterproductive. Like any couple trying to bridge the gap between them, Tyrone and Sharon needed to understand that genuine change occurs gradually. The courage to experiment and take risks, the willingness to be patient, and the compassion to offer support and encouragement are the tools needed to achieve victory.

LESSON ELEVEN: RECOGNIZE WARNING SIGNALS

The love between two people can erode for many reasons. Sometimes, infidelity, sexual incompatibility, or an absence of trust can sever a relationship. The cumulative damage wreaked by less acute but long-unresolved issues can also destroy love. Before conditions deteriorate beyond repair, set aside time to undertake some self-examination and to initiate constructive dialogue. If you recognize any of the following danger signals, your relationship may be headed toward troubled waters.

- You feel emotionally distant from your partner or lonely, even when you are together.
- One of you has begun to spend far more time than usual away from home.
- Your partner's behavior changes suddenly.
- The level of your sexual activity declines markedly.

- You are no longer willing or able to discuss racial issues as they arise.
- You no longer talk about your daily activities.
- Your relationship is imbalanced in some important way, with emphasis placed mostly on your business relationships, your sex life, or your parenting roles, to the exclusion of other areas.
- You or your partner spend more time with a friend of the opposite sex than with each other.
- Minor incidents begin to escalate into big battles.
- You feel humiliated after an argument with your partner.

It is crucial to talk with your partner about any of these warning signals and to state your concerns. Don't make accusations or launch a full-fledged attack. Your objective is to be honest about feelings and foster candid dialogue. In the next chapter, we'll give you a number of communication tools to help both of you get at the roots of your conflicts.

Sometimes, these signals reflect irreconcilable differences. Not all relationships between two people last—and not all of them should. When a relationship becomes emotionally or physically abusive, you need to walk away, at least until your partner has sought help and begun to change. It is harder to decide when to let go of a relationship that no longer feels rewarding but is not overtly damaging either. If you have struggled to resolve your differences and still feel frustrated, unhappy, or trapped in a dead end, you may eventually decide to say good-bye.

In order to separate in a nondestructive way, it helps to be clear about why you are choosing separate paths. A healthy breakup allows you to acknowledge both the good and the painful times you spent together and to move on without recrimination or bitterness. No matter what your complaints, criticizing or blaming your partner offers no rewards.

You should, however, prepare for a period of mourning. The

end of a marriage or a long-term love relationship is a painful loss, even when you are certain you have made the right decision. If your lives have been closely tied together, your emotional investment will not dissolve overnight. Along with maneuvering your way through a web of legal and financial details, you may have to grapple with feelings of failure. If you have children, there may be wrenching custody issues to deal with. You will have to say good-bye to the companionship your partner provided. You may also be divorcing at least part of your social network of friends and family and this loss, too, must be mourned.

The whole process takes its toll, and a period of healing is typically required before you begin to feel good about yourself and ready to rebuild your life. Sometimes, people become involved in safe, but not especially rewarding, transitional relationships once a long-term involvement ends. After he was divorced, George began to date a woman he described as "low maintenance"—she didn't offer him all that much but she didn't make any demands either. He admitted that for the moment he was more interested in companionship and good sex than in emotional intimacy.

Instead of leaping into another relationship, you might take the opportunity of solitude to undertake some self-exploration. Are there things about yourself you would like to change? What would you do differently in another relationship? Have certain negative patterns become apparent? Time devoted to looking inward often pays off—review the self-assessment and self-esteem exercises in this book before jumping back into the dating scene.

LESSON TWELVE: DON'T BE AFRAID TO ASK FOR HELP

Therapy as a tool for attaining self-knowledge and confronting conflict is unfamiliar and threatening to many Black people. You may have been raised to believe that admitting troubles is a betrayal—like other historically oppressed groups, many in our community have learned not to "air our dirty laundry" for fear others will use it against us. If you also feel uncomfortable talking personally to strangers, you may have hesitated to seek professional counseling, or thought of it only as a last-resort measure in a time of crisis.

Quite often, African-American couples come to us seeking help for problems their children are encountering. As we begin to work with them, we often discover the real issues are centered in their own relationship. Sometimes, a couple may even unconsciously foster a problem so that they have an excuse to seek help. This happened with Martin and Cathy, who came in to discuss their daughter Brenda's apparent school phobia. As the sessions progressed, it became apparent that Cathy was actually giving Brenda subtle cues to miss school to force her workaholic husband to become more involved with the family. Because Cathy was unable to confront him directly, she used Brenda as a vehicle to explore family dynamics.

Although we are admittedly somewhat biased on the subject, our view is that asking for help is a sign of strength and courage, not an admission of weakness, and that the support of an objective professional can be very helpful. The willingness to explore your issues, learn more about yourself, confront awkward or unpleasant truths, and work toward change is a sign of courage and commitment. Whether you are involved in a close relationship, or discouraged because you cannot find one, a culturally sensitive therapist who understands the unique psychological needs of African-Americans most likely has something to offer you.

It is best not to wait until an intimate relationship is at the point of disintegration before entering therapy. By then, you may no longer feel genuinely motivated to work toward change. If you are dissatisfied with a repeating pattern, frustrated because you have not been able to ease tensions, eager to resolve a nagging conflict, or hopeful of gaining greater insight into the dynamics of your relationship, a professional counselor may have a role to play. You may also want to consider therapy if you find yourself moving through a revolving door of relationships or repeating self-destructive patterns that prevent you from finding intimacy. A therapist is legally and professionally obligated to keep any information that you share confidential.

If you think a therapist might be helpful, see the appendix for organizations that can make appropriate referrals. Usually, you will receive an initial evaluation designed to help you understand the focus and approach to treatment most likely to work for you. It is extremely important that you feel comfortable and can be open with your therapist. Trust your instincts, and if you don't feel sufficient rapport even after discussing your reservations, don't hesitate to seek another referral.

The Art of Communication: Learning to Talk, Learning to Listen

▲ ▼

Early in a relationship, when you are unfamiliar with each other's communication style and reluctant to create dissension, you may both hesitate to verbalize your true feelings. As you become more intimate, your ability to talk to each other, and to listen, will become more genuine. No matter how long you are together, exchanging confidences and negotiating conflicts will require effort, but the time spent in unproductive or destructive struggle is greatly minimized as your mutual respect deepens and communication skills improve.

Honest communication requires you to tear down the fences you may have erected to protect yourself from pain. This can be challenging to do. Many of the African-American couples that come to our office have had little guidance in the art of self-disclosure and active listening and they need practice. Some of us feel threatened by conflict or are uncomfortable talking about personal issues. If your childhood role models maintained a stony silence when they disagreed or dealt with differences by throwing things at each other, you have been exposed to unhealthy strain and struggle.

Evelyn and David show what can happen to a couple who does not engage in constructive dialogue. Although they have been married for ten years, they never successfully confronted their differing visions for the future. Evelyn dreamed of returning to North Carolina, where most of her extended family still lived; every month, she set aside a chunk of her paycheck, hoping eventually to move south and buy a house. Dave was content in New Haven and not inclined to be especially penny conscious; he mocked Evelyn's dream as impractical and told her she would have to abandon it. At first, a shouting match ensued every time Evelyn mentioned North Carolina. After years of fighting that resolved nothing, the couple ended those ugly scenes by avoiding all talk of the future. They began to withdraw from each other until they were living virtually separate lives. In the place of bitter quarrels, they each carried the burden of silent rage.

When Evelyn and David finally entered therapy in the hopes of salvaging their marriage, layer upon layer of resentment had accumulated. Although they have begun to confront some of their issues, they have a long road ahead. We have been working with them to develop more effective communication skills so that they can find nonthreatening ways to express their emotions. It remains to be seen whether they will take the risks necessary to reestablish the trust and mutual respect that can keep their relationship intact.

Left ignored, unresolved disputes are slow poisons that can destroy a relationship. We hope you will learn to talk long before reaching the sort of crisis that Evelyn and David now face. Honest, direct, and heartfelt communication is one of the foundations of a soul-mate relationship: Disagreements can be healthy and productive when we are willing to engage in open dialogue. To deal with emotional conflicts it is important that we find ways to fight fair, to engage in constructive struggles that do not foster resentment, and to state needs openly, without denying or ignoring your partner's rights.

A LOOK AT COMMUNICATION STYLES

Conflict is an inevitable part of any intimate relationship and should not be interpreted as an indication of incompatibility. The questions of concern are not "Why do we have disagreements?" or "Why doesn't he know what I want?" but rather "How can we resolve our differences appropriately?" and "How do I tell him what I need in a way that is not threatening?"

Moving from hostility to appropriate expression of feelings requires practice. At any given moment, most people tend to communicate in one of four distinct styles. Consider this incident:

You have decided to change your hairstyle. After spending hours at the beauty parlor you come home to model your new hair weave proudly. But your partner is appalled—he doesn't find the new style flattering and accuses you of changing your hairstyle in order to look White. How do you respond?

1. You apologize and offer to take out the weave. We call this a *passive* response.
2. You get angry and say, "Well, the hell with you. I never much liked that mustache of yours, either." This is the *aggressive* approach.
3. You seethe inwardly and say little but plan ways to punish him for his mean remark. This is the path selected by someone who is being *passive-aggressive*.
4. You tell him directly and clearly how you feel, saying, "I'm hurt that you would say that to me. I like my hair this way and it has nothing to do with wanting to be

White. Where is your anger really coming from?" This response is *assertive* and is an effective way to express feelings and thoughts without attacking or withdrawing from others. You invite further discussion and create the possibility of resolving conflicts.

Here's more about each style:

Passive individuals cannot express their feelings openly, and as a result they usually neglect their own needs. They behave in a way that tells the world "Don't pay any attention to me. I need not be taken seriously." They will apologize for their actions, do almost anything to avoid confrontation, and make excuses because they do not know how to be direct. Nonverbal clues—such as a weak voice, the failure to make eye contact, clammy hands, and excess fidgeting—often betray their inhibitions.

One of our clients displayed a typical passive response when her husband wanted to invite some of his buddies over to their house one Sunday night for a game of cards. Martha had a difficult week coming up and was hoping for a little solitude but said nothing about it. Instead, she went out of her way to be accommodating, minimizing her own feelings in the process. Although she was upset about the intrusion on her quiet evening, she suppressed her resentment, telling herself, "I am silly to feel this way."

Aggressive people are often openly hostile or rude in defense of their own interests. Their feelings come first and they go to extremes to make certain they get their way. Tactics used to dominate a partner often include sarcastic responses, put-downs, and shrill verbal attacks. Faced with the card-game scenario, an aggressive person might launch into a tirade: "You never think about what I want. You make me sick. If your friends set foot into this house, I'm going to tell them just where to go." The nonverbal signals of an aggressive response include finger point-ing, talking with the hands, putting the hands on the hips, moving the neck from side to side and scowling.

Passive-aggressive individuals are manipulative and sometimes irresponsible because they are unable to state emotions honestly but are nonetheless determined to get their own way. Rather than saying no or explaining why they do not want to do something, they are indirect; for example, a woman might agree to a request and then do everything possible to sabotage it. A typical passive-aggressive response is for her to arrive late to an event she didn't want to attend or to forget about a commitment she made. A passive-aggressive individual asked about the Sunday-night card game might pout but tell her husband to go ahead with it. If he doesn't pick up on her unspoken unhappiness, she will find a backhanded way to get even—by burning the dinner, perhaps, or searching for ways to disrupt the card game. Body language that often gives passive-aggressive people away includes rolling the eyes, folding the arms across the chest, and sighing a lot. Commonly, passive-aggressives displace anger, lashing out at someone else or overreacting to some unrelated event.

Men and women who communicate *assertively* are most likely to achieve intimacy. Assertive communication does not concern itself with "winning"—the objective is not to overpower or dom-inate—but with laying the groundwork for negotiation. The goal is to express feelings and needs clearly and directly without lashing out or overlooking the partner's viewpoint. An assertive response to the card game might be: "I understand that you would like to have your buddies over for a Sunday-night card game and you are disappointed that I don't want you to." Having restated both positions, you can then assert your own needs. "I have a series of presentations to make at the office next week and I need some quiet to think."

•   •   •

Here are more examples of these four communication styles:

Aggressive	Passive-Aggressive	Passive	Assertive
You made me angry.	Sometimes you are mean to me.	It doesn't bother me.	I feel angry.
That comment was stupid.	That comment does not make sense to me.	Whatever you say is fine.	I feel uncomfortable with what you said.
Get out of my face.	Why don't you go visit your friends?	I'm okay.	I am upset and need time to cool off.
You had better be home by 6.	I am going to start eating at 6.	Whatever time you get home is fine.	I would really like if you could be home by 6.
If you don't call me by 10 P.M., don't call.	I go to bed at at 10 P.M.	Call me any time.	I am looking forward to your call. Please call before 10 P.M.
No!	My feet hurt.	Sure.	No thank you. I don't want to dance right now.

I saw you looking at her, you dog.	Let's go home.	Isn't she pretty?	I feel uncomfortable and disrespected when you stare at other women.

SELF-ASSESSMENT EXERCISE: HOW DO YOU COMMUNICATE?
In order to recognize your own communication style, imagine the following situations and choose the response that most closely matches the one you would most likely make:

1. Your soul mate arrives hours late for a romantic dinner scheduled days in advance. You say:
   a. It's okay, I'll just reheat the food.
   b. I am upset that you were so late.
   c. Where the hell were you?
   d. No big deal, but dinner's ruined.

2. Your partner wants to attend a Kwanzaa celebration but you are only interested in Christmas parties. You:
   a. Attend, wearing a "Celebrate Christmas" sweatshirt.
   b. Refuse to go.
   c. Explain why you do not feel comfortable attending a Kwanzaa celebration.
   d. Go, unhappily.

3. Your soul mate tells you that he is going to a business meeting. Later, you discover he actually met an old girlfriend for dinner. You:
   a. Call his mother.
   b. Cry and tell him how much you love him.
   c. Explain why you feel so angry and disappointed.
   d. Put his clothes in a bag and leave them outside your apartment door.

4. Your soul mate wants to have sex but you don't feel very amorous. You say:
   a. Don't you ever get enough?
   b. I have a headache.
   c. Okay, sexy.
   d. I know that you're in the mood but I'm not feeling like I want sex right now.

5. Your partner wants to borrow $100 but your budget is very tight. You say:
   a. Sure.
   b. No way, you're trying to use me again.
   c. I understand that you need money but I am also on a tight budget and can't spare it right now.
   d. I would lend it to you but my purse was stolen yesterday.

6. You are upset and angry because of a conflict at work and you want support from your partner. You say:
   a. I need a hug, this has been a very frustrating day.
   b. Why can't you be more sensitive?
   c. Let's have sex.
   d. Nothing.

7. Your soul mate goes to a church where people shout when they feel moved by the Spirit. You are used to a more subdued environment and don't feel comfortable at that house of worship. You say:
   a. People at your church act crazy.
   b. I love going to your church.
   c. I would rather not attend your church because I'm not comfortable with all the shouting during worship.
   d. I don't feel well, I can't go to church with you.

8. You always speak in Black dialect but your partner switches up to standard English around White people. You say:
   a. You sure don't have much sense of racial identity.
   b. I feel confused when you change the way you speak.
   c. You speak well.
   d. Next time we see your White friends, I'm going to show them how real Black folks talk.

Here are the communication styles demonstrated by each response:

1. **a.** passive **b.** assertive **c.** aggressive
   d. passive-aggressive
2. **a.** passive-aggressive **b.** aggressive
   c. assertive **d.** passive
3. **a.** passive-aggressive **b.** passive **c.** assertive
   d. aggressive
4. **a.** aggressive **b.** passive-aggressive
   c. passive **d.** assertive
5. **a.** passive **b.** aggressive **c.** assertive
   d. passive-aggressive
6. **a.** assertive **b.** aggressive
   c. passive-aggressive **d.** passive
7. **a.** aggressive **b.** passive **c.** assertive
   d. passive-aggressive
8. **a.** aggressive **b.** assertive **c.** passive
   d. passive-aggressive

Add up the number of responses that fall into each category. Which style do you use most frequently? If five or more of your responses are not assertive, your communication skills may be creating a barrier to intimacy. Commit yourself to learning assertive new ways of talking to your partner.

THE ART OF ASSERTIVE COMMUNICATION

It takes conscious effort to communicate assertively. "Couples often make assumptions about each other's feelings and participate in a process of 'mind reading,' observes psychologist Nancy Boyd-Franklin in *Black Families in Therapy*.[1] "For many Black couples . . . communication and directness in a relationship are very new and uncomfortable. It is, therefore, important to prepare both partners for the discomfort they may feel initially with adopting new patterns of communication. . . . Once they can push past the newness and their embarrassment aroused by these ways of communicating, they will often feel more at ease both with the process and with each other."

Jacki and Max, consummate professionals who have both been very successful in the corporate world, are an example of a couple who never learned to talk to each other. They approach their jobs with an air of confidence and never reveal doubt, moodiness, or personal troubles. Unfortunately, as they rise in the corporate hierarchy, they are finding it increasingly difficult to shift gears at home. They treat each other almost like corporate colleagues, guarding their feelings, glossing over disagreements, and revealing little of their emotional selves. They function most comfortably in a "partner" mode, where they discuss outstanding bills and household responsibilities but nothing more intimate.

As a result, the emotional ties that complete a soul-mate relationship are weakening. In order to reinstate some balance in their lives, Jacki and Max must learn to strip off the character armor they are wearing for the outside world, stop accepting each other's close-mouthed behavior, and begin to communicate in a more direct and revealing manner.

It is important that a nonthreatening climate be established to encourage meaningful dialogue. Nonverbal cues are also an important part of assertive communication. Making direct eye contact, listening attentively, sitting in a relaxed manner, and nodding at appropriate moments all convey a message that you are respectful, attentive, and an open-minded listener.

Too many discussions begin with a negative statement: "We really have a problem" or "You messed up big time." This approach immediately puts the other person on the defensive and heightens a confrontation. Using "I" messages is much more effective: "I need to have more time to myself." "I felt hurt that you did not call me to tell me you were going to be working late." "I feel insecure when you close the bedroom door to talk on the telephone." "It is important to me that you visit my family more often." With an "I" message, you accept ownership of your own feelings while also affirming and validating those of your partner. This sets the stage for candid dialogue.

Here are some positive statements that are useful for introducing touchy issues:

I want us to be even closer . . .
Because I want you to understand me . . .
Although this issue is difficult to talk about, I am raising it because I value you and our relationship . . .
I love you and want to tell you how I feel . . .
I want to understand your point of view . . .

Along with introducing a sensitive subject tactfully, effective communication involves listening without getting defensive. That sometimes means quelling your initially angry response to your soul mate's remarks.

As an example, let us look at what might happen if Betty Ann said to her husband, Harold: "Damn, all those dishes in the sink just make me want to scream." What she really means is, "I am unhappy that you didn't wash the dishes as you had promised," but she is stating feelings in a passive-aggressive, not an assertive, manner.

If Harold feels vulnerable, he might hear an implied attack in her words: "She is telling me that the kitchen is always a mess and it is my fault." His next reaction may be to lose his temper and remind Betty Ann of the time she left all his tools in the backyard where they became rusty.

But with a little effort, he can interpret her remarks in a more positive way. By listening carefully and restating her remark, Harold might say, "So, you're saying that you feel disappointed because I did not clean the dishes as I had promised." This shows Betty Ann that he is trying to be attentive and respect her feelings. It also gives Harold a chance to determine that she is not saying he is a slob or that he never helps with the housework. By restating her remark, Harold becomes convinced that Betty Ann is not launching a broad-based attack on him as a human being and he feels safe enough to concede error.

Sometimes, escalating levels of assertiveness may be necessary. If you are disturbed by your partner's apparent interest in good-looking women on the street, you might first say, "It disturbs me that you stare at other women." If that elicits no response, your next comment might be, "I don't think you realize how strongly I feel about this. Please don't stare." Finally, if you are still not getting anywhere, you may need to say, "I can't be in a relationship where I don't feel respected. It is vital to me that we resolve this issue."

Always remember that you have basic human rights. When you feel those rights may be threatened, reaffirm your rights by repeating the following statements to yourself:

I have the right to my own opinion.
I have the right to be treated with respect.
I have the right to change my mind.
I have the right to say no.
I have the right to pursue happiness.

I have the right to make mistakes and be responsible for them.

I have the right to say I don't understand.

[Adapted from Robert Alberti's "Bill of Assertive Rights"[2]]

THE STAGES OF CONFLICT

Conflicts tend to occur in stages. Often, they begin with an explosion; tempers are hot and neither party is really interested in what the other one has to say. We call this "time to go off." Accusations and blame fly back and forth. During the attack phase, disagreements are exaggerated and damaging statements may be made. A lot of unfair generalizations and "you" statements are spat out: "You never listen to what I've got to say." "You are a liar." "You always take your mother's side against me." Many couples feel uncomfortable with the level of anger that is vented at this stage because it feels threatening. In our experience, however, a certain amount of anger may need to be released before the hard work of genuine communication can begin.

Once the initial eruption is over, the warring parties often separate for a "cool-down" period. One person may storm out in fury. Someone else may disengage, simply refusing to participate in any more heated interactions. However the pitched battle ends, taking a break for a short period of time allows your anger to diffuse and the mood to change enough for more productive dialogue to take place.

Eventually, one of you is ready to make peace and may send a quiet signal of truce. One man we know expressed his regret for an outburst by turning on the electric blanket on his wife's side of the bed so that it would be warm when she climbed in. A woman always made tea when she was calm enough to talk and offered some to her husband in his favorite mug. Along with nonverbal gestures, a simple apology or an invitation to engage in more constructive dialogue is always appropriate: "I know I lost my temper and I'm sorry. I am ready to pay attention and I'd like us to talk things out."

Only when tempers have cooled, and both partners are more open to each other, can real dialogue begin.

We have identified four separate steps that help couples resolve disagreements when they surface. By following these steps, you may be able to skip the stage of explosive conflict, or least minimize it, and move more rapidly to productive communication.

The first step is *awareness*. Both partners must describe the behavior that is of concern and identify their own perceptions of the problem. Rather than making accusations, the goal is to become aware of what is happening and how it is affecting you. As part of this process, you'll both want to understand the depths of your feelings and where they are coming from. Do your responses reflect an off-the-cuff reaction or a deeply held conviction? How much room is there for negotiating? Are your early childhood experiences and personal history intruding on your relationship?

Answering these questions requires some hard soul-searching. In therapy, we may restate comments or ask exploratory questions to foster greater awareness: "Mark, Loretta just said she hates it when you come home from work and ignore her. What are you feeling when you enter the house and see her for the first time all day?" Our goal is to help Mark and Loretta get more in touch with their true feelings and gain clarity about what is really going on in their lives.

Next comes an *information exchange*. Once the sources of tension have been set out on the table, they need to be examined in depth and from every possible angle. Typically, the goal is for both of you to verbalize the thoughts and feelings you may each be acting out but not expressing directly. You will have to be as frank and open as possible about your anger, hostility, anxiety, or sadness. The conversation may become quite heated, especially if one of you says something you really don't mean.

This is often a painful period where you are both likely to feel intensely vulnerable and uncertain about the prospect of overcoming your differences. Active listening allows you to demonstrate your respect for another point of view. By reflecting and paraphrasing a partner's words and point of view, an active listener clarifies them and confirms that the words have been heard accurately. Suppose Pam says, "You never follow through on your promises. You said you would pick up my clothes from the cleaners, and since you didn't I don't have anything to wear."

Steve restates that comment, without adding his opinion. "I hear you saying you are disappointed that I did not keep my promise to you."

That encourages Pam to provide further details about feelings. "Yes, I was counting on you and you let me down."

Eventually, you should reach a place of *understanding*. Now that you know what's wrong, you can begin to share responsibility for your troubles and to acknowledge that you both have a role to play in implementing change. You may still disagree but you have learned where the other person is coming from. For the first time, you are able to validate your partner's feelings.

For example, Loretta may be able to say, "Mark, I can see that you feel pressured when you first come home and I immediately pelt you with questions. I understand that."

Likewise, Steve may be willing to say, "I am sorry I disappointed you, Pam. I did not make picking up your clothes a priority and now I realize that it was important to you. I apologize for not following through on my agreement and for disappointing you."

By expressing empathy for each other's point of view, these couples affirm their willingness to negotiate and to compromise.

Acceptance is the final step. If feelings have been expressed openly, the climate of tension will begin to be replaced by an atmosphere of understanding and respect. The old issues won't vanish but it becomes easier to compromise once destructive patterns have been identified. Couples can also talk about how they make requests—for example, do they ask or do they make demands?—and about the importance of following through on promises. Harold might say, "I will be more direct, rather than agreeing to a request I can't meet." Pam might say, "When I ask a favor from you, I will check to make sure you know how important it is to me."

Rather than trying to convince the other person of the righteousness of your position, you can both become comfortable saying, "We feel differently about this issue and that is okay. You don't have to view the world exactly as I do." At this point, a gesture of good faith and caring is to make a special effort to do something that would please your partner.

Don't get discouraged with this process—it takes a lot of practice!

LEARNING TO GIVE TACTFUL FEEDBACK

When you hold in your emotions, they tend to fester inside and sometimes explode with little provocation or warning. In a soul-mate relationship, you need to let your partner know what you are feeling about yourself, about your relationship, and about him. Constructive feedback builds your partner up; destructive feedback tears him down. Here are guidelines for telling your partner what's on your mind in a clear and assertive manner that doesn't create hostility.

1. Talk about behavior you can see, not what you imagine.
   Destructive: I bet you were hanging out at the bar instead of coming home.
   Constructive: You were not home at eight as you had promised.

2. Don't deal with the "whys" of behavior.
   Destructive: You leave your clothes out because you think it is a woman's job to clean up after a man.
   Constructive: I don't like it when you leave your clothes on the floor.
3. Be specific.
   Destructive: You know I don't like it when you talk that way.
   Constructive: I don't like it when you say I'm acting like a bitch.
4. Don't attack or attempt to humiliate your partner. Focus on behaviors that can be changed, not on personality.
   Destructive: You really messed that one up.
   Constructive: I don't feel comfortable with the way you handled that situation because . . .
5. Don't nag or harass a person about his behavior unless he tells you he wants your help.
   Destructive: How many times do I have to tell you to . . . ?
   Constructive: I'm not sure if you understand how important this is to me.
6. Avoid being accusatory or judgmental.
   Destructive: You make me so angry. You are nothing but a liar.
   Constructive: I feel upset because what you are telling me doesn't seem consistent with what you said earlier.
7. Respect your own feelings and don't blame your partner for them.
   Destructive: You never want to go anywhere with me and you don't care how that makes me feel.
   Constructive: I feel sad because you don't want to go with me to the party.

8. Don't be sarcastic or condescending.
   Destructive: Let me know next time you can fit me into your busy social calendar.
   Constructive: I feel rejected when you cancel plans at the last minute.
9. Talk about how you feel instead of offering unsolicited advice.
   Destructive: You should have told your boss to do the job himself because you had other plans.
   Constructive: I felt frustrated when your boss pressured you into working on Saturday.
10. Focus on the present; don't rehash old conflicts.
    Destructive: I bet you got the telephone number of that woman at the party, just like you did last month.
    Constructive: I felt threatened when you spent so much time talking to that woman at the party.
11. Be sensitive to your partner's feelings, not critical.
    Destructive: Why do you always . . . ?
    Constructive: I need to tell you how I'm feeling because it bothers me when you . . .
12. Avoid confrontation when emotions are running high but express feelings as soon after the incident as possible.
    Destructive: Last month, when you made the comment about my weight, I wanted to punch you in the mouth.
    Constructive: I was so angry earlier today when you commented about my weight that I couldn't talk without getting aggressive.
13. Be direct; don't let your feelings be filtered through a third party.
    Destructive: My mother was upset because you didn't buy me anything for my birthday.
    Constructive: I am upset with you because you didn't buy me anything for my birthday.

14. Give your partner a chance to express opinions.
    Destructive: I don't care how you feel.
    Constructive: How do you feel?
15. Focus on your soul mate's positive traits.
    Destructive: You are finally starting to listen to me.
    Constructive: Thank you for listening. I feel much better when we communicate, even if we disagree.

LISTENING UP

Listen when your partner talks to you. That may sound obvious, but when a couple is dealing with sensitive or aggravating subjects it is very easy to tune your partner out or become defensive. Asking for feedback, and paying attention when you get it, is possible only in an environment of trust and respect. If you don't understand something, say so. Ask for time to think about an issue more thoroughly, but be sure to follow up on it.

Here is help in really listening:

1. Be open and receptive.
   Cutting off communication: Why would you say such a thing?
   Open listening: Please tell me what you think.
2. Don't make excuses.
   Cutting off communication: You don't know what you are talking about. The reason I didn't go to your office party was because I had nothing to wear.
   Open listening: I appreciate your sharing your opinion with me, although I see the situation differently.
3. Value your partner's opinion.
   Cutting off communication: I don't care what you have to say.
   Open listening: It is important that you tell me what you think.

4. Express gratitude and appreciation for your partner's concern.
   Cutting off communication: Who are you to tell me that?
   Open listening: Thank you for caring enough to tell me what you think.

5. Discuss things thoroughly.
   Cutting off communication: I heard you, now let's drop the subject.
   Open listening: Can we talk about it some more?

6. Engage in follow-up discussions.
   Cutting off communication: I don't want to talk about this ever again.
   Open listening: Let's continue to discuss this periodically.

7. Develop a personal action plan for taking feedback to heart.
   Cutting off communication: You are making that up, I never roll my eyes.
   Open listening: I will become more aware of how I roll my eyes when I am talking to you.

8. Don't be hostile.
   Cutting off communication: You think you know everything.
   Open listening: I am listening to what you are saying and trying to understand.

9. Don't be vindictive.
   Cutting off communication: Since you are so eager to tell me about myself, let me tell you a thing or two.
   Open listening: I feel upset hearing what you have to say, but I want to be clear about your point of view.

10. Don't look for hidden agendas.
    Cutting off communication: You are just trying to find a way to hang out with the guys and pick up women.

Open listening: I hear what you are saying about needing some time for yourself.

11. Restate messages to clarify what is being said.
    Cutting off communication: So, you don't want to be with me anymore?
    Open listening: Are you saying you don't want a commitment?

12. Reflect on what you are being told.
    Cutting off communication: You made your point but I don't see it that way at all.
    Open listening: I think you have a point. I've never considered the situation in that light before and I'd like to think further about what you are saying.

13. Don't think about how you are going to respond once your partner is finished.
    Cutting off communication: I thought it over already and my mother was right.
    Open listening: I hear you saying you were upset when my mother intervened in our argument.

14. Don't insist on having the last word.
    Cutting off communication: That's just the way things are going to be and I don't want to talk about it anymore.
    Open listening: I hear what you are saying, although I still disagree. Let's discuss this some more tomorrow.

CONTRACTING WITH YOUR PARTNER

Negotiating a contract with your soul mate can be a very effective way to identify specific problems and come up with a strategy for resolving them. Sometimes, a couple has an initially negative reaction when we suggest drafting a contract. "This isn't a business, it is a marriage," one man told us. We agree, of course, but our experience has shown us that contracting is a terrific tool for cultivating the marriage garden. By working together toward a shared vision, you remind each other that your relationship is important enough to warrant improvement. As a result, you may both begin to feel more loved and to act in a more loving way even before you have fulfilled all the terms of your contract.

Try to schedule contract negotiations when neither one of you is under pressure so that you do not feel rushed. Contracting works best when both parties sincerely want to make changes and can be quite specific about goals. An objective such as "communicate better" is too general and too hard to measure. Much better is, "Let's each cook at least three times a week," "Let's take a walk by ourselves for at least one hour a week," or "Let's visit my family once every two weeks for at least two hours." Here's how to negotiate a contract in a climate of safety and trust:

Step one. Before you begin, list all the things you enjoy about each other. This builds up a reservoir of good feeling and creates a positive atmosphere that allows you to listen to each other.

Step two. Make a list of the issues you aim to address. Be as specific as possible. Then choose one or two to tackle first, preferably the easiest ones. Once you see how effective contracting can be, you will have more confidence to tackle the thornier problems. For example, Maynard might complain about Lisa's tendency to collect stacks of magazines in every nook of their apartment, while Lisa might express her frustration with Maynard's chronic lateness.

Step three. Define your goals. Maynard wants to find a way to reduce the clutter. Lisa wants to know when Maynard will be home.

Step four. Describe how you will work to resolve your problems. Lisa might promise to devote an hour each weekend to sorting through her piles and agree to keep only those publications she really wants. Maynard may agree to post a note prominently in his office that reads, "It is getting late. Did you call Lisa?"

Step five. Agree that you will both acknowledge your appreciation for the other person's efforts. Maynard might tell Lisa, "I noticed that the pile of newspapers in the bedroom has dwindled. Thanks for sorting through them." Lisa might say, "I really appreciated your telephone call last night, Maynard. Thank you."

Step six. Determine a schedule for reviewing the contract. It is important to assess your progress and check in with each other to make sure the arrangements are working as agreed.

Step seven. Fill out the contract form, sign and date it. These may seem like unnecessary formalities but having an official document will increase the likelihood that you take it seriously.

A sample contract follows:

This contract is made between soul mates _____ and _____ with the goal of resolving certain sensitive issues between us and improving our relationship.

These are the problems we will focus on for the next month:
1.
2.
3.

Our goals for these problems are:
1.
2.
3.

Specific ways we will work on these problems are:
1.
2.
3.

Both parties agree to comply with this contract to the best of our ability. We will sit down in our family room together every two weeks on Sunday afternoon to review our progress and determine whether the contract is working. This contract can be renegotiated at any time, at the request of either party.

_____   _____
NAME   DATE

_____   _____
NAME   DATE

SEVEN GOLDEN COMMUNICATION RULES

Whether you are trying to resolve an issue that caused one of you to fly off the handle, asking your partner for something you need, or introducing a sensitive topic, the basics of effective communication are the same. Sometimes, *what* you say is a lot less important than *how* you say it. Here are seven golden rules for saying it right:

1. **Initiate dialogue.** Although it may seem easier to ignore conflicts than to try to resolve them, wounds left to fester never heal properly and will eventually undermine a relationship. Hold fast to a vision of yourself as a peacemaker, someone who is eager to reach a place of understanding. Choose the appropriate time and place in which to start difficult conversations.

2. **Listen actively.** Use both verbal and nonverbal signals to let your partner know that you are focusing undivided attention on what he has to say. Repeating his words—"You are saying that you'd like me to tell you more about my day at work"—is one way to underscore your attentiveness and to encourage him to volunteer more information. Asking open-ended questions that cannot be answered with a simple yes or no also lets him know you really want to understand what is bothering him. An example: Rather than asking, "Did you have a good day?" you can express

greater interest by saying, "Tell me about how things went for you today."

3. Validate feelings. Your partner's genuine emotional responses deserve respect. Feelings are never right or wrong; they simply reflect a person's subjective experience. If she says, "I feel rejected and think that you don't want to include me in office parties," it is unfair to say, "You are silly to feel that way." Allow her to own her feelings. Support her by saying, "You are telling me you feel excluded."

4. Don't interrupt. While your partner is expressing her point of view, limit your comments and questions to what is needed for purposes of clarification. Otherwise, the message you send says, "What you have to say is not as important as what I have to say." Your turn to offer a more detailed response comes later.

5. Stay on the subject. Don't drag in other grievances or old hurts into current conversation. Resolve one conflict at a time.

6. Fight fair. No matter how angry you feel, never deliberately hurt your partner. There is nothing more destructive than focusing on his vulnerable spots or making nasty comments about something you know he is sensitive about. Long after an argument is resolved, the raw wounds inflicted by those cruel words will linger. Speak carefully and don't go on the offensive.

7. Respect differences. No matter how articulately you state your position, you may not be able to convince your partner to see things your way. Sometimes, a conflict can only be resolved by an agreement to disagree.

PART IV

▲ ▼ ▲ ▼

CONFRONTING THE TOUGH ISSUES

▲ ▼ ▲ ▼ ▲ ▼ ▲ ▼ ▲ ▼ ▲ ▼ ▲ ▼ ▲ ▼ ▲

CHAPTER SEVEN

The Enigma of Sex, the Risk of Infidelity

▲ ▼

Now that you've had some training in communication skills, put it to good use by dealing assertively with some of the sensitive issues that almost all soul mates face at one point or another. These include sensuality, sexuality, and infidelity; work and money; ethnic identity; and family and spiritual life.

We'll address sexuality first. Physical intimacy, which is a means of expressing emotional attachment, sharing pleasure, and stating commitment, is central to a soul-mate relationship. As one client said: "There is magic to sex when there is an emotional bond as well as a physical one. When two soul mates touch each other in an intimate way, you can feel the other person's inner being and experience both joy and sadness, pain and moments of ecstasy. We come together in a way that transcends the sexual; it is as if our souls have merged."

Lovemaking is usually a barometer of a healthy relationship. Do you trust each other? Are you able to reveal your vulnerabilities? Have you honed your communication skills and learned to compromise? Is there a genuine give-and- take that satisfies you both? If the answers are yes, the chances are good that you will be able to let down your guard and enjoy physical intimacy. But if there are impediments to your emotional rapport, or you are feeling uptight about other parts of your life, problems may become apparent in the bedroom. Until you get at the source of your sexual troubles, you are likely to feel vulnerable and insecure about your relationship.

Amanda and Douglas have established an admirable level of intimacy that allows them to express their love fully. They are comfortable with their own bodies and take enormous pleasure in lively sexual play. Sometimes, they express passion with steamy, erotic sex; other times a tender touch is all they use to communicate abiding love. They enjoy experimenting and don't fear failure, knowing if one new sexual position doesn't work well, there are plenty of others to try. Both in bed and out, Amanda and Douglas listen well and communicate frankly, constantly renewing their commitment to each other as they find new ways to enhance physical and emotional intimacy.

In order to duplicate their accomplishments, we'll look first at why there can be trouble in the bedroom and then at what you can do about it.

WHAT INTERFERES WITH GOOD SEX

Sexual dissatisfaction can assume many faces. Some African-American men and women complain that their partners don't want to have sex often enough; others say they want it all the time. Some say there isn't enough affection or sensual arousal before intercourse. Others complain of partners who demand too much of both. Men often say: "My woman never initiates sex. I always have to make the first move and see whether or not she will push me away." Just as frequently, a woman will say, "My man only seems to be concerned with pleasing himself in bed.

I enjoy good sex as much as he does but I wish he'd involve himself a little more with my needs." Another remark that may sound familiar is: "The sexual chemistry just isn't there between us but at least I know I can count on him."

If you are single, sex introduces a unique set of challenges. You may feel pressured to sleep with a man soon after you start dating to stave off rejection, or you may confuse sexual desirability with your sense of worth. After her longtime boyfriend broke off their relationship, Inez felt betrayed and her self-esteem took a nosedive. To assure herself that she was still desirable, she jumped into bed with every man who expressed any interest in her. Until her bruised confidence began to heal, Inez had trouble saying no, whatever her real wishes.

The immediate problems in the bedroom usually have their origins somewhere else. Whether you are just getting serious about someone or have been involved for years, guilt, stress, depression, anxiety, parental attitudes, religious conflicts, social stereotypes, and doubts about self-worth can all impede sexual response. The loss of desire for sex can also reflect unresolved sexual differences between two people.

Often the sources of dysfunction can be traced to troubled childhoods and the absence of self-esteem. It is hard to express sexuality in a full and uninhibited fashion when you hear your parents whispering that sex is "nasty."

When Christina came into therapy, she admitted she did not like to make love with the lights on and was acutely uncomfortable with oral sex. Her husband resented her sexually repressed ways and their marriage was floundering. In order to change, Christina first had to understand why she felt so anxious and tense in bed.

In Christina's case, her mother used to say, "Only girls from the projects enjoy sex," and she had come to believe men would lose respect for her if she enjoyed physical pleasures too much.

As a result, she was holding herself back. In therapy, we encouraged her to erase the old messages, and her girlfriends chimed in with their own blunt advice. "Girl, you go out and get yourself a sexy negligee and let that man know he turns you on," said one. Christina was open to new ways of expressing her sexuality, and slowly her mother's words lost the power to hold her back. She was astonished at the improvement in her marriage.

Another impediment to good sex is body image. If you have internalized messages that suggest, "You are too ugly to attract a man," or "You are too dark to turn a woman on," you learn to dislike your own body. This self-doubt then prevents you from becoming aroused by your partner's touch. You may even minimize your attractiveness by wearing unflattering clothing or carrying a lot of excess weight. By telling others to "stay away," sexually repressed people avoid confronting their own issues. To appreciate your distinctive beauty and open yourself up sexually, you must once again find ways to make peace with your past.

The voices of the church can also leave a legacy of guilt. If your minister kept warning you not to be promiscuous, the message you internalize may be that it is "a sin" to enjoy sex. Recently, we counseled a couple who felt a conflict between their sexual desires and their belief that premarital sex was immoral. Both of them had waited a long time to find the right partner and were afraid their relationship would not last if they repressed their sexual urges. We helped them understand that emotional intimacy can precede physical intimacy and encouraged them to continue exploring their personal priorities in therapy. Their strongest need was to prevent sexual ambivalence and religious guilt from destroying their relationship.

The traumatic experience of sexual abuse, no matter how long ago, can also disrupt healthy sexual adjustment. This act of violence can shake your confidence and fill you with guilt, self-loathing, and fear. It also leads some individuals to act out sexual anxiety through promiscuity. One woman we saw in therapy was unable to have an orgasm. We traced her troubles to an encounter with an uncle who had sexually aroused her as she slept. She had awakened to the sensation of an orgasm and as an adult still confused the pleasures of sexual fulfillment with the shame of that experience. To experience intimacy now, she had to make the difficult commitment to confront the realities of abuse and move beyond them.

Impediments to sex may also be associated with workplace or family pressures. Anxiety about a job, money, parents, children, other personal relationships, or almost anything else can erupt in the bedroom. A man who feels uptight may be unable to have an erection. A woman who cannot stop worrying is unlikely to relax long enough to have an orgasm. Fears about sexually transmitted diseases, including AIDS, can also interfere with pleasure, although a commitment to safer sex—by using condoms and having fewer sexual partners—can reduce the risk.

Sometimes, alcohol or drug use is the culprit in sexual problems. Although many people use these substances to relax or to enhance sexual performance, they may actually have an opposite effect. Used in excess, alcohol and drugs induce a chemical imbalance that can impair judgment and reduce physiological responsiveness. Especially in the presence of anxiety or depression, substance abuse can even result in temporary impotence.

Donna and Harry entered therapy in an effort to rekindle some sexual excitement in their relationship. Their once excellent sexual rapport had vanished and weeks went by without physical intimacy. It soon became apparent that Harry was bringing his professional frustrations home. When he had first signed on at a multinational securities company, he had been an ambitious go-getter, but as the company's preference for White managers over Black ones became apparent, Harry grew frustrated. Although he was not in a financial position to jump from the corporate ship, he began to approach his job with lethargic indifference. The absence of stimulation left him feeling bored, and that translated into a loss of sexual appetite.

Some men express frustration in just the opposite manner, using sex to express their power or to compensate for their feelings of failure. Because they feel impotent in the workplace and have no way to assert themselves, they insist on proving their manhood in the bedroom.

SELF-ASSESSMENT EXERCISE: SEXUAL HANG-UPS

Here's an exercise to help you assess whether you have a sexual hang-up:

1. Do you have sex less frequently than you would like?
2. Do you have sex more frequently than you would like?
3. Do you think oral sex is dirty?
4. Do you ejaculate prematurely?
5. Do you feel guilty or anxious about sex?
6. Do you always prefer to have sex in the dark?
7. Do you usually need a few drinks before you can have sex?
8. Do you have difficulty telling your partner what you like and dislike in bed?
9. Do you rely heavily on sex toys or vibrators to enjoy sex?
10. Do you always wait for your partner to initiate sex?
11. Do you have to wash immediately after sex?
12. Do you avoid afterplay, going immediately to sleep instead of talking, bathing together, or cuddling?

If you answer yes to two or more of these questions, you probably need to devote some energy to exploring sexual issues. Whether the roots of your sexual problems rest in painful childhood experiences or in contemporary stress, you'll need to confront them in a similar way. The first step is to identify the sources of conflict. Are they lodged in the early messages you heard about sex? How was the subject handled in your home? Did you learn that physical intimacy is an expression of emotional closeness or that sex is dirty? How do you experience sex today? Is the sexual side of your current relationship significantly different from previous sexual involvements? Were you more satisfied with one partner than another?

The next step is to figure out what the answers mean and relate them to your present difficulties. Have the messages of childhood made you uptight in the bedroom today? Does a precipitous decline of sexual interest suggest your current relationship is not right for you? Are you allowing workplace stresses, financial worries, or other anxieties to enter the bedroom and interrupt pleasure?

Finally, develop a concrete plan of action. If you are being held back by old voices, take a look at the section on making peace with your past in chapter 3. It is time to replace negative messages with positive self-statements, such as: "I'm a healthy sexual being and I am entitled to physical intimacy." Perhaps your search for answers revealed that you are not communicating well with your partner, that you are distracted by financial worries, or that you are not fully committed to your current relationship. Before sexual communication can improve, you will have to start dealing with more fundamental issues.

Other tips for changing your sexual perceptions:

- Learn how to relax. Meditation, deep breathing, and exercise help allay feelings of anxiety.
- Read books about human sexuality that encourage you to accept and enjoy a healthy sexual response.
- Get to know your own body. Touch yourself in different places, and in different ways, to discover what you enjoy most.

- Write down your concerns and feelings, and the circumstances when they arise. Discuss them with your partner or a trusted friend.
- Consult a therapist who has expertise in sexual issues. The associations in the appendix can direct you toward someone who is reputable.

ARE YOU BLINDED BY GOOD SEX?

After that lengthy discussion about sexual incompatibility, it may seem that many couples aren't having too much fun in bed. But in some relationships, the issue is just the opposite—you may not be dissatisfied with your sexual rapport, just everything else in your relationship. Have you ever said, "That man sure knows what to do in bed but we never talk" or commented, "That woman sure is hot, but I can't bring her around to the office. She's not exactly the corporate type"?

Sexual compatibility can sometimes mask an absence of emotional or intellectual rapport. David and Brenda seemed to be totally turned on to each other. They went everywhere hand in hand, patting each other on the backside, and kissing passionately in public. In bed, they were just as hot, spending hours making love almost every day, exploring each other's bodies, trying new sexual techniques, and trying to please each other in every way imaginable. Brenda was so turned on by the scent of Dave's cologne mixed with his perspiration that she slept in his undershirts when he was out of town as a way of feeling close to him.

But they had no common ground outside the bedroom. Brenda dreamed of going back to college to become a nurse but never spoke a word about it to Dave. Dave was worried about his elderly parents, but Brenda didn't know anything about their health problems. Their sexual chemistry was unbeatable, but they couldn't talk to each other. They knew how to be lovers but not friends or partners. For their relationship to last, Brenda and Dave need to find more in common than good sex. Just as emotional intimacy is incomplete without a sexual expression of love, so sex is less satisfying unless it is accompanied by emotional intimacy.

Sometimes, abstinence can be the best way to find out if a strong sexual connection is interfering with your ability to make wise judgments. This may be appropriate if you are considering ending a relationship or uncertain how deeply involved you wish to become with someone new. Declaring a time-out prevents the intimacy of sex from becoming distracting, allowing you to clarify your feelings and make the decisions that are right for you.

TALKING ABOUT "IT"

In the bedroom, as elsewhere in our lives, we must learn to talk to each other and to listen. Many of us become frustrated and angry when our partners do not give us what we want in bed—unfairly, we expect them to read our minds, and when they can't, we become resentful. No matter what the source, sexual problems can poison a relationship if there is no dialogue.

Let's say the cause of your partner's diminished sexual appetite is trouble at work. If he can talk about it, you have an opportunity to express empathy—"I hear you say that you're feeling too stressed to have sex right now. I understand how that feels and I can accept it." Suppose, however, that he can't verbalize his feelings. That forces you to guess about what's really going on, which means your own insecurities are likely to surface. You may interpret his absence of interest as a personal rejection or as a sign of an affair. If you are not communicating clearly, you may make wild accusations that cause your partner to become defensive. As a result, an issue that initially had nothing to do with your relationship creates tension and anger.

In long-term relationships, another challenge is to avoid taking your soul mate for granted. Suppose you met a woman to whom you were really attracted or a guy who turned you on in a big way. Would you let weeks go by without expressing any interest? Would you withhold gestures of affection every time she walked into the room? Would you shirk from sex most of the time because you were "too tired" or not interested?

Probably not, yet this is just what some people do after they have been together for a while. As the years pass, they stop thinking of soul mates in sexual terms and start viewing them more as buddies or colleagues. Fantasies may evaporate and sex becomes routine or infrequent. Gone are the sexy lingerie, the scented candles, the sensual foreplay, the unexpected afternoon bout of lovemaking. It doesn't have to be this way but you'll have to work at breaking old habits; good sex doesn't happen without effort. Rekindling the sexual fire that once burned between you requires inventiveness and a willingness to be adventurous. Here are some rules for maintaining the edge of sexual excitement in your relationship:

Allow time for lovemaking. If sex becomes just one more thing you have to do, it is going to feel more like a time-consuming obligation than an expression of deep intimacy. Try going to bed before you are tired or making love on weekend mornings when other pressures do not impose themselves on you quite so intensely. Although you may desire spontaneity, scheduling special days for sex allows you to look forward to it all day and cuts down on frustrations and guesswork in a relationship.

Remember that variety is the spice of life. Make sex a little more unpredictable. Whether you experiment with new positions, vary the time of day that you make love, or move out from the bedroom into the living room (or the kitchen or the dining room, if you feel like it), don't have sex at the same time, in the same place, and in the same way every time. Not everything you try is going to work equally well, and that is okay—the idea of experimenting is to find out what you like.

Add sensuality to your sex. Be creative in finding new ways to relax, enhance your sense of well-being, and stimulate eroticism. For some couples, incense, soft lights, massage oils, gentle music, or a warm bath can be terrific turn-ons. Others enjoy sharing their fantasies or playing games with each other; we know one married couple who likes to pretend they are involved in an illicit love affair. Anything goes between two consenting adults so long as their activities take place in an environment of mutual respect and no one gets hurt.

Ask for what you need. Sometimes it is a little embarrassing to state sexual preferences explicitly. You may also be fearful that your partner will think you are challenging his or her technique; actually, our clients tell us they genuinely want to know what gives their partners pleasure. "I don't find it threatening when a woman tells me what she wants," said one man. "It can be helpful as long as her approach is right. Someone who says, 'I'm going to have to get you together here, brother, so you can do this thing right,' is not going to do much for my self-esteem. But if she says, 'Maybe we can try this,' or 'I prefer this instead of that,' it can definitely improve things between us."

Using "I" messages—"I really like it when you do this" or "I feel uncomfortable when you do that"—instead of "you" accusations—"You're not doing it right"—is the best way to get what you need. Approach the subject with tact and sensitivity and be sure you both understand that the goal is to improve your sexual compatibility and pleasure.

Respect your partner's efforts to change. It is not easy to alter one's sexual approach and it is important to support your partner for trying. When Mark complained that Genevieve was too passive in bed, she made a conscious effort to make love differently. Instead of validating her, he then complained, "When she tries to be more sexual, it feels artificial to me. I think she is just faking pleasure." That perspective denies Genevieve respect for her efforts. Even if it feels a little mechanical, Mark needs to acknowledge and thank her, recognizing that in time, and with appropriate support, her approach and efforts are likely to become more spontaneous and natural.

Don't blame yourself for your partner's sexual difficulties. If a partner brings sexual baggage from the past into your relationship, try not to let it make you feel anxious or inadequate. When Robert first began dating Mary, he discovered she was unable to have an orgasm without using a vibrator. Initially, he viewed this as an obstacle he could overcome with resourceful sexual techniques. After a few months, he became frustrated. "I don't know what else I can do to get her to enjoy sex with me," he complained. The answer: relatively little. Mary had to take responsibility for exploring the sources of her repressed attitude, which were most likely lodged in childhood, and for working through them. Robert's role was only to support her and encourage her to seek help; he could not take responsibility for making her more sexually responsive.

Be alert to shifts in sexual appetite. If you are making love less frequently than you did in the past or sense that you are not enjoying sex as much as you did, don't ignore the message. When a partner withdraws sexually, it may reflect external pressures, emotional factors such as ambivalence about the relationship, or even an affair. Instead of jumping to conclusions or pretending a problem doesn't exist, insist on talking about what is really going on. Remember, however, that it is normal to go through periods of being less sexually active as long as they are not prolonged.

THE GOLDEN RULE: BE FAITHFUL

Infidelity is one of the most serious threats to a stable relationship that most couples will face. A soul-mate relationship is fundamentally about trust; when an extramarital affair is revealed, the security of a solid foundation is shaken. The sense of betrayal and knifelike pain that accompany the discovery that your partner has been sexually intimate with someone else leaves a deep, slow-healing scar that is not easily repaired.

In our view, genuine commitment is impossible without monogamy. When you decide to be faithful, you say, "This is the relationship that I am going to work at right now. I choose to refuse other sexual opportunities, no matter how harmless or how appealing they may seem to me." This is not always easy to do. At first, you may feel that you are saying no to all sorts of potentially exciting possibilities, and that's scary. But if your quest for a soul mate is genuine, you will find that monogamy carries its own rewards.

Contrary to myth, infidelity is not a man's exclusive province, but our counseling experience does suggest male infidelity is more common, probably because society still views it as more acceptable. There are many reasons for infidelity. Some people crave sexual excitement or a renewed sense of romance (the reason most often given). Others are looking for the emotional intimacy that is lacking in their present relationship. An affair may be used to escape boredom or a sense of routine, or to experience the high that comes from tasting forbidden fruit. Some people turn to illicit love affairs seeking an ego boost or a way to counteract low self-esteem. On a less conscious level, others may be trying to shine a spotlight on their own marital troubles by sending a message that says, "We are ignoring our conflicts. Perhaps doing something dramatic outside this relationship will force us to deal with them."

Whatever the motivation, infidelity is usually a signal of a communication breakdown. Peter told us that he had been driven into the arms of another woman because his wife was indifferent to sex. He said he had tried to arouse her interest with erotic talk and gifts of perfume and negligees but she remained cool to him. "She cares more about being with her girlfriends than devoting any energy to my needs," he complained.

Sylvia's interpretation of their problems was very different. "Peter is always pushing me to have sex. When he brings me presents, I feel like I'm being bribed—here's a bottle of perfume, now you owe me a sexual favor." She found his erotic talk embarrassing instead of a turn-on. "My mama taught me that I'd get my mouth washed out with soap if I talked the way he does," she said. "And I spend a lot of time with my friends because I need someone to confide in. Peter sure isn't there for me."

Because the channels of communication had become clogged, Peter and Sylvia each put the worst possible spin on the other person's behavior. Sylvia felt cheapened by Peter's efforts to arouse her, and Peter felt spurned and resentful. To break the impasse and stop rehashing the same arguments, they needed to air their grievances, validate each other's feelings and intentions, and clarify their own.

Black men and women are no more or less likely to be unfaithful to each other than other couples, but there are some distinctive psychological and historical dimensions to the infidelity within our community. Perhaps you grew up in environments where monogamy was rare. In your family and the surrounding community, affairs outside the marriage bond may have been tacitly accepted. One man we know recalls his father taking him to his girlfriend's home and winking as if to say, "Don't let your mother know where we have been." Some of our female clients remember being given a different message in childhood: "Don't worry if your man steps out every now and then. The important thing is that he supports you and the family. If you make a big deal out of it, you might drive him away." Some Black writers have even claimed this behavior is appropriate, arguing that "man-sharing" is a legitimate solution to the surplus of Black women.

Nancy and Kwame, who had been married for five years when they came into counseling, illustrate the impact of family influences and the value of assertive communication. When Kwame began to have a series of short-term affairs, Nancy refused to stay silent. Instead, she issued an ultimatum: "You either stop seeing other women or I'm gone." Kwame wanted his marriage to endure but revealed his fear that sexual fidelity was not masculine behavior. This message had been conveyed by his father, who often boasted about his many sexual conquests, and by his grandfather, who had secretly maintained a second family. With these adult role models dominating the landscape of his childhood, it was not surprising that Kwame believed desirable Black men have more than one partner.

In therapy, Nancy made clear that her threat was real. At first, Kwame professed astonishment that she would make such an issue of his philandering, which he viewed almost as a hobby. "You know you're my main woman, Nancy," he said.

Nancy refused to be mollified. "It just hurts too much to know you're in someone else's bed, Kwame. I'll walk if you don't quit and you'd better know I mean it."

By refusing to "enable" Kwame's behavior by ignoring it or excusing it, Nancy succeeded in bringing the issue to the negotiating table. Confronted with the prospect of losing the woman he loved, Kwame began to think differently about fidelity. He admitted that he had not considered fully how his affair would impact on the trust and commitment that are crucial to marriage. Despite the models of relationships with which he was most familiar, Kwame was able to recognize that soul mates must sometimes sacrifice things they want in order to get things they really need. By dealing with their issues in an open and non-threatening way, Kwame and Nancy were able to rebuild trust and renew their pledge of commitment.

WHEN YOU DISCOVER AN AFFAIR

Whether you stumble onto an affair accidentally or your partner confesses, the discovery often causes anguish and rage. The shock of betrayal may cause the wounded partner to wonder whether the caring and closeness that once seemed so real were actually a charade. No matter how long a couple has been together, the entire foundation of a relationship is likely to be called into question. The revelation of an affair is like the convulsions of an earthquake—once the ground stops shaking, nothing feels quite so secure again.

That's what happened to Martha and Al, who had been married ten mostly happy years. One evening, during an intimate conversation about the marital troubles of a friend, Al confessed to a casual and short-lived affair many years earlier. He thought his admission would be no big deal to Martha because it had happened so long ago, but Martha grew pale at the news. When the shock subsided a little, she said furiously, "How could you have done such a thing? What other secrets are you hiding from me?"

Al tried to reassure her, insisting the affair had been a one-time-only event that long since faded in memory. Martha refused at first to listen to his explanations or apologies and scoffed at his pledge to prove his loyalty in any way he could. After weeks of treating him coldly, Martha finally shared a story about her parents' unhappy marriage that Al had never heard. "When I was little, I saw my mother suffer in silence as my dad moved from one affair to another," she said. "I vowed that I would never tolerate a man who was unfaithful to me."

That insight helped both of them understand her intense reaction to Al's story, but the process of healing and rebuilding trust still did not happen overnight. Like most couples dealing with the aftermath of an affair, Martha and Al had to embark on a long struggle to renew and restore their soul-mate bonds. The mending took place little by little, day by day. Open communication, a willingness to forgive, and faith that real change is possible are the tools that can salvage a commitment. Here is a road map back from infidelity:

Admit that an affair is taking place. Before you can expect to alter behavior, you must acknowledge what is really going on, stop tolerating it, and begin the struggle toward change. Too many people deliberately ignore or even deny the truth. Rather than provoking a confrontation, they engage in a conspiracy of silence in which direct questions never get asked and flimsy excuses go unchallenged. A couple's codependent bond allows them to pretend a relationship is healthy even though they know it is not.

For months, Nina had colluded with her husband, Joe, who began having an affair shortly after he was laid off from work. The terror of being left alone stopped her from a direct confrontation. Instead, she internalized her pain and began drinking heavily to fight a mounting depression. The couple sought counseling only when the tension in their marriage began to manifest itself in the behavior of their children.

In therapy, Joe and Nina finally acknowledged the affair and linked it to the loss of self-esteem that accompanied his job loss. "I felt like a failure because I could not provide for my family," he said. "I just needed to get away from home sometimes so I could leave my concerns behind." Only by admitting the truth, instead of playing a game of pretend, could Joe and Nina move toward renewed intimacy.

Put a halt to an ongoing affair. Before you are ready to do the work necessary to repair your soul-mate bonds, an extramarital affair must come to an end. Expecting to restore intimacy while sustaining the affair is like expecting an open sore to heal even though you keep scratching it.

Think about why monogamy is so important. Some of our clients manage to convince themselves that an affair will not detract from their primary relationship but only enrich their own lives. We have often heard people say, "This has nothing to do with my love for my wife. It is just that my girlfriend fills other needs." In our experience, that attitude is not realistic. The features of a healthy, intimate soul-mate relationship—trust, candid communication, shared vision, and commitment, among them—simply can't be sustained without fidelity.

In one of our discussion groups, a man named Paul tried to justify his infidelity by linking his behavior to the practice of polygamy in some parts of Africa. Another discussion group participant called Paul on that comparison. "Get real, man. America today is nothing like Africa of yesterday. The Black sisters I know have too much self-respect to tolerate that line. You all know what rules apply now." We agree. Although many of our African legacies are inspiring, not all the ways of the past have relevance today. Taking responsibility for our lives as Black people in twentieth-century America means letting go of traditions that are no longer appropriate.

Deal with your issues. It is important that you understand why someone has had an extramarital affair. Were the roots of infidelity lodged in work frustrations, misguided anger, resentment, low self-esteem, or some other issue external to the relationship? Or was it a cry for help ("Our relationship is in trouble and this is the only thing I can do to get your attention")? Whatever the underlying issues, they must be confronted honestly—if the conditions that led to infidelity are not addressed or the anger of the wounded party is allowed to fester, no healing can take place. It may be wise to seek professional help—a neutral third-party counselor can offer insights into your troubles and help you negotiate your differences. Too many couples blame each other for an affair and may need help learning to take responsibility for their behavior, regardless of what prompted it to take place.

CHAPTER EIGHT

Frank Talk About Work, Money, and Power

▲ ▼

Assertive communication is also an effective tool for diffusing the tension often associated with jobs, money, or the division of household tasks. If we are lucky, our accomplishments at work make us proud. Learning to be good at something we enjoy, winning accolades from our colleagues, and making enough money to feel comfortable and to enjoy some of life's pleasures reinforce a sense of self-worth and bolster our confidence. When we feel good about ourselves, we feel more secure about what we can offer others, and that, in turn, makes us more attractive to prospective soul mates.

But the extent of our career achievements, earning power, and status, and the way these impact on the division of household tasks, can sometimes complicate African-American relationships. "All I want is someone who has a job," said a woman in exasperation. After years of dating men who worked sporadically, if at all, she had defined stability as an essential characteristic of a soul mate. "Never mind his politics, forget who his mother is.

Right now I just want to see that steady paycheck. Until I do, I'm content to stay single."

Our friend Eldridge felt equally frustrated by the dating scene, where he kept meeting status-conscious women who seemed more interested in his paycheck than his personality. "Image is what so many of these sisters seem to be all about. They like flashy cars and expensive clothes. I'm not really sure whether they care about me or just the money I make."

Some men and women moan that it is hard to find a partner who is their intellectual equal, while others wish a soul mate's professional commitments didn't interfere with the time allotted for intimacy. Many single women complain about men who are too focused on their careers, while quite a few men worry that ambitious women won't make room in their lives for a family. Money is another frequent source of conflict—some couples fight constantly about earning money, spending what they have, and coping with outstanding debts.

Markedly different perspectives about education, work, money, or the division of household tasks can sound the death knell for a relationship. If your priorities are worlds apart—if there is no shared vision—your bonds aren't likely to last. But if you share at least some of the same attitudes, you may be able to overcome your differences. Here is a look at the issues that divide brothers from sisters and how you can deal with them.

How Our Attitudes Are Formed

Like any expression of personal values, attitudes toward economic and job-related accomplishments begin to evolve in childhood. Whether or not your parents had the privilege of formal schooling, many Black people learn to value education from an early age. If you were imbued with the idea that education is the road to achievement and that working hard is the best way to attain your vision, you are likely to seek a partner with the same outlook.

Your perspective will more likely be very different if you grew up among kin who minimized the importance of schooling. A client of ours named Joe was a good student, but his parents kept warning him not to set his sights too high. "You don't have to go to college," said his mother. "That's for White folks." Those expectations discouraged Joe from devoting himself to his studies or making the sacrifices necessary to pursue a degree.

Similar messages shape our view of money. Some of us were raised in households that were perpetually in debt. It seemed that no matter how good the times, or how bad, our families lived beyond their means. Every penny anyone earned was spent immediately; credit-card debts mounted until the limits were reached; and there was no such thing as a savings account. In other households, the rules were very different—we learned to buy only what we could afford and somehow managed to set aside a little money every month, no matter how low our family's income.

Such childhood experiences can affect adult soul-mate relationships in unexpected ways. Morris, for example, was raised by a single mother who held down a full-time job outside the house. She worked hard, clipped coupons, counted pennies, and kept the household together by sheer determination. At a very young age, Morris and his brother did most of the cooking and cleaning and knew that their contributions were crucial to the family's survival. Morris grew into an extremely reliable and hard-working adult with a carefully laid-out career path, a very cautious approach to money, and a distaste for frivolity. His highly developed sense of responsibility leads him to be overprotective, yet ironically Morris is attracted to assertive, independent women— women very much like his mother—who insist they can take care of themselves. Conflicts surface because Morris needs to be in charge and feels uncomfortable when his dates won't allow that.

• • • •

Because most of the economic power in the United States is concentrated in White hands, some of the experiences that shape our views toward work and money are unique to African-Americans. Studies consistently show that Black men at every level of education earn much less than their White counterparts, whether they have dropped out of high school or completed graduate degrees. Access to good jobs remains limited, and in many corporations there are ceilings above which Black people have never been promoted. No matter how talented we are, we may have to work twice as hard to advance half as far.

Thus, the workplace is likely to be as much a source of frustration as one of satisfaction. Many Black people hold on to secure jobs, even those they dislike, because they are reluctant to risk a steady paycheck. Chuck, for example, wanted to start his own business, but he was apprehensive about investing in the new venture and leaving his job. He kept remembering how his mother used to say, "Don't take any chances. You get yourself a good situation and hold on to it. There's a lot of people doing without and you don't want to join them."

Chuck's wife, Bernadine, who had grown up in a more financially well-off home, believed it was sometimes appropriate to sacrifice security to pursue a dream. A true soul mate, she inspired Chuck with her confidence and encouraged him to stretch beyond what was safe and secure so that he could grow. "I've got a good job that I enjoy, Chuck," said Bernadine. "It feels like the right time to take a risk in our lives. If you don't go for it now, when will you be able to try again?"

DECIDING WHAT YOU WANT

Understanding your own attitudes toward work and money can help you decide what is important in a soul-mate relationship. There are no right or wrong answers, only choices that work best for you. Do you want to be with someone who has an impressive record of professional accomplishment? Lots of money? A good education? Can you be happy with a partner who is not very ambitious? Someone who won't do any of the household tasks? Your priorities will reflect the expectations with which you were raised, your own needs, and the vision you hope to realize.

Some Black men and women care deeply about finding a partner who has attained a comparable level of education and professional success. "I want to be with a lady who knows how to speak well and moves comfortably in the White world," said Sam, who is an accountant. "I'm expected to attend a lot of corporate functions, and someone who is not at ease in that milieu will reflect poorly on me."

Others seek a traditional partnership in which the woman runs the household and is not heavily invested in a profession, even if she works to bolster the family income. Daniel, for example, broke off a relationship with a career-oriented woman to marry someone whose primary goal in life was to take care of her man and to raise children. In therapy, Daniel admitted that he still had strong feelings about his ex-lover but felt that in the long run, he would be unhappy with a professional who could not devote herself primarily to home and hearth.

Some brothers and sisters place greater emphasis on the ability to form close emotional ties or to pursue spiritual interests than on financial and professional accomplishments. "I don't care about a man's salary," said Mara, who complained that in some professional circles men and women practically exchange résumés before going out on a date. "I'm looking for someone who has a sense of himself and is willing to make a commitment. His job doesn't mean much to me because I earn a good wage and I can take care of myself."

Sue, a television producer, had a different perspective. She entered therapy to talk about the experience of dating a cabinet-maker with little formal schooling. Although he treats her well and they have a close emotional bond, she felt frustrated by his lack of intellectual interests and kept pushing him away whenever he talked about a more exclusive commitment. "I really care about George, but I just don't know whether we can make it last," she told us in counseling. "I worry that I will feel limited or constrained by him somewhere down the line."

There are healthy reasons for choosing someone who is not your professional equal—and there are unhealthy reasons as well, so it is important to understand your own motivations. If you are involved, or looking to get involved, with someone of lesser educational status, ask yourself these questions:

- Am I intimidated by someone who has more education than I do?
- Am I looking for the ego boost that sometimes comes with being more successful than my partner?
- Am I settling for someone who does not challenge me sufficiently because I am afraid of being alone?

If any of the answers is yes, you may have some self-esteem problems that require attention. But if you can truthfully answer no to each one of these questions, by all means cultivate any relationship that works for you. Single people who do not automatically spurn the attentions of those who are less professionally accomplished can select from a larger pool of soul-mate candidates.

Here are some questions to ask if you are only interested in dating people who are upwardly mobile:

- Is money more important to me than emotional intimacy or a shared vision?
- Am I looking for a prosperous partner so that I do not have to be concerned with my own development?
- Am I overly interested in what my friends and my family think about my choice of a soul mate?

Again, yes answers may be cause for concern, but the green light is on if you can say no to all three questions.

Who's Got the Bucks?

Another sensitive issue facing many couples is what to do when a woman is bringing home the larger paycheck. In a society that views money as synonymous with status and power, insecure men may feel that their masculinity is threatened. "I don't want to compete with my lady," a client named Luther said. "When my dad lost his job and my mother had to support the family, his ego was shattered. I'm not about to re-create that experience in my own life."

How earning power affects a relationship will depend on the people involved and their willingness to discuss a tough subject. Soul mates need to talk honestly and to confront any ego problems that surface. When Althea got an important promotion, she said to Jake, "I've never earned more money than you do. Let's discuss our feelings about this."

At first Jake made light of the subject, claiming, "I think it is great that my woman can support me." With gentle prodding from Althea, he finally admitted to underlying feelings of inadequacy. Althea listened attentively and mirrored his words back: "I hear you saying that perhaps you are not living up to social expectations."

Then, she told Jake how she felt. "I hope we will not be confined by other people's standards. I know you make many important contributions to the household and I'd like us both to enjoy our extra money."

Jeanette and André are an instructive contrast, a lesson in what *not* to do. Jeanette regularly reminds André that her wages make their life-style possible and hints that he is a failure. When the couple entered treatment, Jeanette mocked him for his failure to contribute to the household. "He's never been worth much," she said bluntly. "He dropped out of college and I've been doing more than my share ever since." Rather than protesting Jeanette's assessment of him, André at first seemed willing to accept it. Only after months in therapy could he admit that he felt demoralized; it took Jeanette just as long to understand how she used her income as a weapon in their marriage.

Sometimes, a woman's greater financial resources can highlight other tensions in a relationship. When Cara got an inheritance from her aunt, unresolved issues of sexual intimacy suddenly came to the fore. Cara had never confronted her distaste for sex, which could be traced back to her mother's not-so-subtle message that "good Black women don't enjoy sex." Cara had viewed sex as an obligation, and when she became financially independent felt that she no longer "owed" it to her husband, Billy. In response, Billy swung alternately between states of withdrawn depression and demanding hostility. Cara tried to appease him with expensive presents, but Billy's craving for emotional and sexual intimacy eventually led him to the arms of another woman.

In this example, money was not the central problem but the fuel that fired a different conflict. To restore emotional candor and sexual health to their lives, Cara and Billy have to confront both personal and interpersonal issues exposed by the inheritance windfall.

Rose and Manny are another couple whose communication problems were accentuated by income differences. Rose has a graduate degree and an executive-level corporate job; Manny, who has not completed college, works as a low-paid office clerk. They came into therapy to discuss conflicts about child-rearing techniques, but other issues quickly surfaced. Manny complained that Rose was encouraging their daughter's pretensions, while Rose criticized Manny for being a poor role model for the seven-year-old girl.

"Your backwater southern roots are pulling us down," Rose charged. "I'm tired of being with a man who doesn't provide for his family. You've had plenty of chances to improve yourself but you haven't taken advantage of them. I don't want my daughter thinking that you are all that a Black man can be."

Manny's response to Rose's hostility was to mock her professional successes and to discourage their daughter from practicing the grand piano Rose had so proudly purchased. He told his wife, "I'm not going back to school to earn more money so that my daughter can have more expensive music lessons. What's next? Ballet and acting classes?" The couple was locked in a vicious cycle of combat—Rose berated Manny, Manny lashed out, and Rose redoubled her criticism. They were unwilling to call a time-out and talk frankly about their different priorities. In therapy, it became apparent to them both that their relationship was over. We guided Rose and Manny through the difficult process of letting go, while encouraging them to do some internal work to prevent similar conflicts from surfacing in their next relationships. We also helped them address coparenting issues so that they could share in the responsibilities and pleasures of raising their daughter without putting her in the middle of their conflicts.

GETTING AND SPENDING

Along with earning power and professional accomplishments, spending habits can lead to big clashes. If one partner is a spend-thrift and the other a careful saver, it is very difficult to work toward a common vision. A single mother struggling to support two young children is not going to feel comfortable with a man who likes flashy clothes, expensive cars, and partying all night. "I've got to see that steady paycheck," says Martha. "I work too damn hard to put up with someone who is not together enough to get a job."

Likewise, a man who is building a business is going to have

a hard time with a woman who demands a Mercedes Benz and a mink coat. Jason and Shelly had been dating just a few months when Shelly hinted that she hoped to have a fancy new car every couple of years. Jason thought that goal was frivolous and told her so, but she adamantly disagreed. "I decided long ago that's what I want and I'm going to have it," said Shelly. "And I'm going to find me a man who wants it just as badly as I do." Her words were a clear signal to Jason that he could not forge soul-mate bonds with Shelly.

American consumer society encourages us to accumulate new possessions, even if we have to buy them on credit. The self-esteem problems that afflict some in the Black community may make us especially vulnerable to advertising campaigns that equate status with the size of our cars, the cut of our suits, or the electronic equipment we own. By saying, in essence, "You are worthwhile only if you wear expensive clothes and have a fancy car," these ads encourage people to ignore internal qualities and evaluate themselves and their potential partners by the value of their commodities.

When Clara met David, he owned both a sports car and a Cadillac and was about to buy expensive leather furniture for the suburban house he had purchased a year earlier. Although he made a good income, Clara soon discovered that David was always behind on his bills and had creditors breathing down his neck. He didn't seem disturbed—in fact, he loved to browse expensive shops in search of new things to buy—but Clara knew their relationship was not going to last. "He doesn't understand that he has to work and sacrifice to get what he wants," she said. "He wants it all now even if he can't afford it. I can't handle that way of thinking."

If you feel that an intimate relationship is jeopardized by chronic economic pressure or dramatically different attitudes about getting and spending, it is important to face your issues and get down to an honest dialogue about money. Here are some strategies for coping:

- Choose an appropriate time to talk about finances. Avoid raising the subject when the bills are due and the stresses of living on a tight budget are especially apparent. A more conducive opportunity might be when one of you gets a raise or you start discussing some major new purchase.
- Talk about your short-term and long-term financial goals and try to develop a plan for meeting them. What do you really need? What do you really want? Make an effort to distinguish genuine desires from the status-building possessions a consumer society encourages you to buy.
- Expect the unexpected and prepare for it. Layoffs have become frighteningly common. Illness can never be anticipated. The decision to have children invariably wreaks havoc on the family budget. Instead of stretching your spending to the limit, try to put some money aside so that life's twists and turns do not throw you completely off course.
- Don't use money to manipulate your partner. Offering bribes in the form of expensive presents to attract a partner, or to keep one, reveals low self-esteem and is demeaning to you both.
- Don't be blinded by the size of someone's paycheck, no matter how large or small. Although money has a very real place in our lives, it should not be the sole measure of a person's worth.
- Never use earning power as a weapon in an argument. A bigger paycheck does not entitle anyone to more control over the relationship. Soul mates are equal partners, regardless of who earns more.

BRINGING IT ALL BACK HOME

Even if you don't have a financial worry in the world, you are unlikely to be immune from workplace stress. Anyone can have a bad day at the office, but African-Americans often face the added burden of racism, and this can put tremendous strain on soul-mate relationships.

Regardless of our professional success, we are sometimes overlooked by our White colleagues. Many of us have had the experience of making a comment at a meeting that is ignored until someone else rephrases it—and gets praised for the insight. Or we may feel that we are being asked to do more than our fair share of tasks and wonder how we will be perceived if we assert ourselves by saying no. Will our colleagues think we are not team players? Will we help fuel the stereotype that Black people are lazy and shiftless? If we agree to do more than we consider reasonable, will we invite further exploitation? Will passive acceptance convey a message that we do not have the pride or self-confidence to speak up for ourselves?

It is almost impossible to check these concerns at the front door of your home. Unless you process your emotional response to a workplace problem appropriately, you can easily displace feelings onto an unrelated situation. For example, the sense that you are invisible or not valued on the job may make you extremely sensitive to rejection from a lover; a feeling that you have been exploited at work can make you unduly sensitive to inequities in how household chores get done.

Martha sought therapy after her husband told her he didn't want another child. Rather than experiencing his decision as an expression of financial realities and his own emotional needs, she saw it as a personal rebuff. In counseling, she said: "Ralph doesn't want me to be the mother of his children." By exploring feelings, she was able to trace the real source of her insecurities to work, where her talents had not been sufficiently rewarded.

This insight positioned her to view both Ralph's decision and her work problems more realistically.

Sometimes, workplace stress manifests itself in a drive for conquest. Men, in particular, use this curious logic: "The boss may not respect my talents, but my address book is filled with women's telephone numbers. That means I am worthwhile and desirable." Worse, feelings of powerlessness may emerge as self-destructive behavior or bullying. A man who does not derive a sense of accomplishment at work may be overly aggressive at home, telling himself, "At least I'm in control here."

The impact of job pressures is often more indirect. For example, Nancy, a powerful advertising executive, had a tight grip on the reins of power in an intensely pressured field. Whether she faced an impossible deadline or made a presentation to secure a multimillion dollar account, Nancy remained calm, rational, and decisive. No one who worked with her—her subordinates, the board of directors to whom she was accountable, or her competitors—doubted for an instant that she was in complete control.

But she had become so adept at controlling her emotions that she was unable to release them at home. Nancy was attracted to men who were in awe of her and withdrew if they sought her softer side or challenged her dominance. Despite her Superwoman image, Nancy revealed in counseling that she was terrified of professional humiliation. Her image of perfect control, carefully cultivated to prevent her colleagues from discovering secret fears, had become an unintentional obstacle to her ability to have a soul-mate relationship.

It takes emotional security and conscious effort to deal with work stress frankly. Soul mates can help. Joseph was bitterly disappointed when he learned he was not going to get the promotion he expected. At first, he refused to talk with his wife, Angela, about this acute blow to his self-esteem. "It really doesn't matter much," he claimed, but his angry tone of voice revealed it mattered a great deal.

Angela was sensitive to Joseph's real needs, offering him support without being heavy-handed. "Joseph, I hear you saying that the promotion was not very important to you but it seems to me you are very disappointed. I care about your feelings and would like to hear them. Why don't we go into the living room and talk about it?" By assuring Joseph that his feelings mattered and that it was okay to be disappointed, Angela extended the support he needed to release his bottled-up frustrations and then to identify the next steps.

The moral: If you are experiencing difficulties on the job, as Joseph was, it pays to open yourself up to someone who cares about you and ask for support. If you are involved with someone in pain, as Angela was, extend a hand and let your soul mate know you are there to help. The ensuing dialogue can bring you much closer.

WHO WILL COOK AND CLEAN?

When both partners are making important economic contributions, household chores can become a flashpoint. In some homes, Black men share responsibility for shopping, cooking, cleaning, and child care, but more often, traditional men expect women to carry more of the daily load, even if they both work full time.

The division of labor has been a source of tremendous tensions in Shelly and Leon's household. Shelly holds a rank in her corporation that is higher than any previously attained by a Black woman. Leon, who is a successful academic, boasts to his friends about her achievements but tells her, "My woman has to run her house as well as she runs her company." Shelly is torn between Leon's expectations, which echo the traditional messages she has gotten from her family, and resentment about being expected to play Superwoman. They bicker constantly about the chores.

Arguments about division of labor surface for many reasons. Men who were pampered as children may now look for partners who will cater to them in the same selfless way their mothers did. Others seek an antidote to the harsh treatment they receive on the street and in the workplace by demanding first-class service at home. The cultural mores of White society depicted on television and on film also foster sexism. Although the Ozzie and Harriet model doesn't reflect reality in the contemporary White world anymore—and never conveyed life as it is for Black people—it creates an "idealized" image of how things should be.

At a workshop we held for single men and women, a discussion about the legitimacy and limitations of traditional roles became quite heated. It began when one man asked innocently, "Doesn't a woman take some pride in preparing dinner for her man? Or fixing him up a nice plate of food at a party?"

There was a chorus of nos from the women and then a young attorney explained how she felt. "I don't mind fixing you a plate one evening if you'll do it for me the next time. The problem for most of us is your expectations. We don't think women should always be doing the cooking and catering."

Added another woman, "I really object when you tell me that I derive pleasure from this. You are putting words into my mouth. You might like it, and I might decide that I'll do it for you, but I don't want you telling me how I should feel about it."

As with most potentially divisive issues, there is room for negotiation when a climate of trust exists, as our friend Melvin discovered. In his family, the women traditionally prepared plates for their men and he loved the special treatment. His wife, Ellen, came from a family with no such custom. Melvin told her: "This makes me feel good. If we're in this relationship to uplift and nurture each other, then can you do this for me?" After discussing the symbolism they each associated with the gesture, Ellen agreed to accommodate Melvin's desires by serving him at parties. But Melvin appreciated the fact that she was making a sacrifice for him, and they both knew that he would also have a turn at pampering her in a manner that she desired.

There is no ideal way to share tasks, but both partners must feel comfortable about the arrangements they make. Personally, we favor an equitable division of labor. As Haki R. Madhubuti notes: "It is insensitive and callous for men to expect their wives or mates, who often work eight hours, to come home and cook the food, clean the apartment, feed their children and husbands, do the dishes, mop the floors, wash the clothes, and perform other household chores. If Black women are to advance and develop, they need time for self-realization. The sharing of housework does not diminish a man's masculinity; rather, it affirms a man's sense of fairness, love and security."[1]

In our own lives, we find that an equitable division of labor sets a wonderful example for our children by demonstrating the value of everyone's contribution to the household. Shared tasks also reinforce the link between cooperation and intimacy that is so crucial to soul mates.

Dealing
with Race

▲▼▲

Racial issues are another hot button that can explode into conflict unless soul mates can talk about them. The way we view ethnic identity, interracial relationships, and racism reflects both our own upbringing and experiences and the attitudes of our community. Once again, it is not necessary for couples to deal with these issues in exactly the same way but it is crucial that they understand and respect each other's perspective.

NEGOTIATING CULTURAL DIFFERENCES

Conflicts frequently arise when one member of a couple travels exclusively in Black circles while the other tries to live a genuinely multicultural existence. This was the case with Matt and Nancy. Nancy was fiercely committed to empowering the Black community and when Matt became the first person of color to become a member of an exclusive tennis club, she considered it an act of betrayal. "Don't you know you're just their token nigger?" she asked with rage. "Now they've got one Black face they can point to if anyone squawks about discrimination."

Matt saw things completely differently. He was thrilled to be granted the privilege of membership, taking it as a sign that he had finally arrived and as a first step toward paving the way for more Black members. He felt stung by Nancy's criticism and the conflict left both of them feeling wounded and misunderstood.

For a relationship to work, it is not necessary that a couple define themselves as African-Americans in precisely the same way but they must both feel comfortable with their heritage and be able to respect whatever accommodations their soul mate has reached. "If she wants to pierce her nose and wear African garb but doesn't have any problem with me wearing a suit and tie most of the time because that is how I feel comfortable, then we have no problem," says Walter, a broker at a major Wall Street firm. "But if she expects me to get my nose pierced, it is not going to work."

As culturally sensitive therapists, we are persuaded that African-Americans feel best about themselves, and are most likely to be victorious, when they nurture ancestral traditions while respecting their connections with America and learning to relate comfortably to people with different heritages. W. E. B. Du Bois called this the "duality" of Black existence in White America.

We introduced Tina, an entrepreneur who built a small business from scratch, to the concept of duality in order to provide a fresh perspective on a fledgling relationship. Tina had been raised to believe that equal opportunities were available to anyone willing to work hard and hates to be defined as a "Black executive." When she came to us for counseling, she said she was dating a physician whose acute sense of ethnicity made her feel uncomfortable. "His apartment is decorated with African statues, he only listens to jazz, and he insists on calling himself an African-American. This obsession of his interferes with our relationship."

Tina claimed that she was at ease with her own racial identity but felt it was something to accept, not to emphasize. "It's like being left-handed," she said. When she talked about her upbringing, however, it was obvious that some conflicts remained unresolved. Her mother had downplayed the legitimacy of a distinct African-American culture and taught Tina that assimilation was the best way to achieve material success. In an example of how we sometimes look for partners with characteristics opposite those of our parents, Tina was often attracted to strongly Black-identified men.

In time she began to understand that it was not necessary to minimize the importance of her African heritage nor to immerse herself exclusively in things Black, as if she had to prove something. Having previously assumed that she had to come down firmly in the camp of either the Black or the White worlds, Tina found duality to be a real awakening.

Hard experience has taught that when we emphasize our common humanity to the exclusion of our ethnic heritage, Black people are forced to adapt to White norms. In a society where we seldom get to establish the rules, asserting "We are all the same" really means "Let's all be White." For African-Americans, that means living forever in gray shadows.

However, we don't think there is a place for an anti-White attitude that allows us to judge others or to spurn them because their traditions differ from our own. As long as they do not demand that we adhere exclusively to European norms, and we do not expect them to become immersed in African-American culture, White friends, clients, and colleagues can enrich our lives. The key to maintaining successful personal and work relationships is to be genuinely respectful of one another's traditions and the perspectives they provide while acknowledging and accepting our differences and viewing them as a source of strength, not a reason for divisiveness.

Navigating the sometimes rocky course between two worlds is not always easy. Barbara and Eric, White friends of ours who are Jewish, were visiting us at our Connecticut home shortly after the black activist leader Reverend Jesse Jackson, for whom we have great respect, made a remark that was widely criticized as anti-Semitic. Although we objected to Jackson's comment, we nonetheless defended his long track record and his commitment to the Black community. We moved into some very sensitive issues as we sat around our kitchen table talking about the growing tensions between Blacks and Jews. Because a high degree of intimacy and trust had been established over the course of a long friendship, we were able to speak frankly and to admit how vulnerable the subject made us all feel. Although our interpretation of certain issues differed, we found areas of agreement and closed the dialogue with enhanced feelings of mutual respect.

Your own ability to accommodate duality depends mostly on personal experiences. Someone who grew up in segregated neighborhoods or suffered the anguish of racist attacks may find it difficult to trust White people and choose to the greatest extent possible to work and socialize in an all-Black world. By contrast, a person who was raised in an integrated environment may more readily welcome interracial friendships and work ties to the White community.

For Marilee and Clyde, these differences have become a source of tremendous struggle. Clyde is the only Black account executive in an aggressive young advertising agency that has been designated as "one to watch" by a major business magazine. He works long hours and centers his social life around work. After he had a long telephone conversation with his boss one evening, Marilee exploded with anger. "When you get on the phone with those people, you talk differently. I've watched you at office parties trying to act White. You'd best remember who you are because you're never going to be accepted in that world."

Clyde was furious. He prided himself on his ability to relate to White people but was also involved in Black causes and felt quite comfortable with his ethnicity. He thought that Marilee was judging him on shallow terms and was blind to the legitimacy of approaches that differed from her own.

Sandy and Bernie are able to handle similar differences much more effectively. When we first met them, we were struck by the contrast between them. She is a highly articulate bank vice president who is always perfectly manicured, enunciates her words carefully, and is accustomed to traveling in White circles. Bernie's real passion is poetry, although he worked at odd jobs to pay the bills. He dresses casually, speaks in language rich with Black idioms, and hangs with an artistic set. Yet they have been able to bridge the gaps because of their profound respect for each other's unique talents. They do not criticize each other or try to alter the other person's approach to the world. Instead, they find ways to deal with differences that leave them both feeling whole.

Sandy and Bernie's story illustrates the compromises that are possible and necessary, especially when you are moving up the ladder in a corporate environment while your Afrocentric soul mate is focused completely on Black traditions. A common problem you may face is what to do when you are expected to socialize with your business colleagues. One option is simply to attend certain professional events by yourself. An alternative is to ask your partner to accompany you, while making it clear that you do not expect him to deny his true self. If that's what you agree on, check in with each other during the event to make sure you are both feeling comfortable.

The specific solutions are less significant than the way you approach the issue—as always, affirmation, respect, and assertive communication are the tools that work best.

THE HIDDEN TRUTH ABOUT SKIN COLOR

Along with learning to accommodate the mainstream world, coming to terms with racial identity means thinking differently about your own brothers and sisters. An open secret in the Black community is the existence of a status line dividing men and women with light skin, straight hair, and thin lips from those with darker complexions, broader noses, full lips, and "kinky" hair. The many variations in between only complicate matters further. In order to tear down this impediment to mutual respect and love, we must first acknowledge the distorted lens through which we sometimes view one another. As we become more aware of the "color consciousness" that has existed in the past, we can more readily stop perpetuating this ignorance.

Until Emancipation, Blacks folks whose skin color or facial features suggested some Caucasian ancestry were viewed by their owners as genetically superior to those with very dark skin and "negroid" features. Generally they were assigned domestic chores, rather than field work, and allowed to interact directly with White families. Special privileges, such as the opportunity to learn a craft, were often bestowed on them and they were usually first to be offered their freedom. After the Civil War, light-skinned Blacks found work more easily and had easier access to education, a pattern that has only gradually begun to change.

Many Black people have accepted these externally imposed standards of beauty. In the 1920s, upper-class Black clubs applied a "blue vein" standard of membership—you'd be allowed through the doors only if the blue veins in your forearm could be detected. The paper bag test and the comb test were variations on the same theme—if your skin color was lighter than a brown bag, if you could run a comb smoothly through your hair, the club was open to you. There were also Black fraternities and sororities that have historically accepted members according to skin tone.

This began to change during the Black Is Beautiful movement

of the 1960s, when Afro hairstyles came into vogue and many of us began to appreciate the full spectrum of Black beauty. For a time, the pendulum even swung so far in the other direction that very dark-skinned Blacks claimed to be the sole legitimate heirs of African traditions. Some of our brothers and sisters took a "Blacker than thou" attitude that erected another, equally destructive, barrier between our people. Sadly, a fully enlightened perspective still eludes us. When we look closely at the people of color featured in fashion advertising, music videos, and television broadcasts, we see that, for the most part, light skin is still considered highly desirable and dark skin remains less valued. Even young children are aware of societal attitudes toward skin color. In our book *Different and Wonderful: Raising Black Children in a Race-Conscious Society*, we discuss research in which we asked Black children: "Which doll has a nice color?" Sixty-five percent of the children chose the White doll over the Black one.

The more we are inundated with mainstream society's portraits of what is desirable, the more likely we are to absorb and internalize that standard. The booming business in hair relaxers, bleaching creams that claim to lighten skin tones, and cosmetic surgery that alters the shape of our noses and lips all attest to our dissatisfaction with physical features that hearken back to our African homeland. A similar outlook is reflected in the attitudes of both genders. "I never date dark women," said one of our clients. "They just don't seem to turn me on."

Family members also influence our concepts of beauty. One man remembers how cold his father was to any dark-skinned woman he dated. His unspoken message was: "Don't get serious about this lady. I don't want dark grandchildren." Sometimes, the issue is framed in practical terms—a mother might emphasize the economic advantages likely to accrue by marrying a light-skinned man. However it is phrased, the message is the same: The European look is good, the African look is bad.

Skin color can foster a special crisis when children are involved. For example, one of our clients told us that her husband accused her of having had an affair when their light-skinned son was born. Another woman sought counseling for a severe case of the "baby blues," known clinically as postpartum depression, after the birth of her dark-skinned daughter. Pat, who is also dark-skinned, talked with great anguish about how detached she felt from both her husband, Charles, who has light skin and wavy hair, and from their baby.

We helped Pat link her disappointment with the infant's appearance to her own negative self-image. The shame she felt about producing a child with features like her own also made her feel unworthy of her husband's affection and sexual attention. Once the real issues had been clarified, we could explore the messages Pat had heard in childhood and adolescence and help her understand that a narrow view of physical beauty was cutting her off from a loving marriage. Although she could not shake off her deeply ingrained attitudes about racial features overnight, becoming aware was an important first step for her.

To break free of these sorts of limiting stereotypes, African-Americans need to examine their own prejudices and define more inclusive standards. The key lies in taking pride in our diversity and becoming curious about the rich heritage that has given us so many differing appearances. Perhaps the man with dark skin tone is a descendant of an escaped female slave who fought off the white man's sexual advances. The Black sister with the almond-shaped eyes may have a fascinating story to tell about the marriage between her Chinese grandfather and her black grandmother. Perhaps the brother with a prominent nose has some Cherokee Indian blood coursing through his veins. When we see these looks as a legacy of our complex history on American soil, we can begin to celebrate our differences, instead of rejecting or criticizing them.

Remember, you are not at fault for internalizing negative messages about your own appearance and skin color or the appearance and skin color of the partners to whom you are attracted. These have been imposed on you since childhood. But as a self-aware adult, you can take three steps to rid yourself of the blinders you may be wearing. First you can recognize the presence of inner voices telling you what makes a Black brother or sister beautiful. Second, you can understand how external standards have distorted your perceptions. And finally, you can strive to shed preconceptions, biases, and stereotypes so that you can see yourself and others more clearly. In this way, you broaden the pool of potential soul mates, bolster your own self-esteem, and provide a model for your children and the generations of Black youngsters to follow.

SELF-ASSESSMENT EXERCISE: IDENTIFYING YOUR OWN BIASES

Here is an exercise to help you see whether you have internalized any of the racist messages about Black men and women that are conveyed both in our own community and in the White world. Honest answers will help you identify your own biases and recognize thought patterns that distort your vision.

Mark each item according to this key:

> A. I never think that way.
> B. I rarely think that way.
> C. I occasionally think that way.
> D. I often think that way.

> 1. Lighter skin is more attractive to me than darker skin.
> 2. Straight hair is more attractive to me than curly hair.

3. Thin lips are more attractive to me than full lips.
4. Thin noses are more attractive to me than broad noses.
5. I am unlikely to be turned on by someone with pronounced "negroid" features.
6. Most Black families are matriarchal or headed by females.
7. Most Black men and women have affairs even if they are involved in a committed relationship.
8. Sex is the most important part of most Black relationships.
9. Most Black men are untrustworthy.
10. Most Black men are emotionally or physically abusive.
11. Most Black men are lazy.
12. Most Black women are untrustworthy.
13. Most Black women want to dominate their men.

Scoring:

A. One point
B. Two points
C. Three points
D. Four points

13 to 26: You have not internalized racist messages.
26 to 39: You may have internalized racist messages and should devote some energy to exploring your attitudes and feelings with someone you are close to. Try to work toward dispelling myths and developing more informed and positive attitudes.
39 to 52: You have internalized many racist messages about Black men and women and may need to seek professional help in sorting them out.

To understand more about how you have internalized racist messages, answer the following questions and discuss your responses with a trusted friend.

1. Did any of the questions to which you gave a C or a D answer create tension in your current or most recent love relationship? How was the disagreement resolved?

2. Describe any specific experiences that help account for the C or D answer. Is there a link between that experience and any difficulties you have had in a relationship?

3. Can you identify a characteristic in your current or most recent partner that supports your C or D answer? Is there a characteristic that contradicts it?

4. Can you identify a characteristic in yourself that supports your C or D answer? Is there a characteristic that contradicts it?

TALKING FRANKLY ABOUT RACISM

Even if you are not biased yourself, you must still operate in a world where discrimination is an all-too-frequent occurrence. In order to process the rage, embarrassment, and sadness that accompany racial insults, you must talk openly about them and ask your soul mate for support.

It pays to be mindful about where your frustrations really lie and avoid displacing them onto someone else. One afternoon Shirley had a nasty conflict with her boss at work; she felt exploited and confronted him about being given more work than her White colleagues. Their discussions had not gone well and she was steaming with anger when she came home and faced her household chores. As she began folding the laundry, resentment toward her husband began to build. Her first words to Norris when he walked in the door were, "I do all the washing, why can't you ever help put the clothes away?"

What she really meant was, "I have had an infuriating day and feel that I am being mistreated at work. I need to know that you won't take advantage of me, too. Please reassure me." Norris, of course, had no way of knowing that and immediately became defensive, which only made Shirley feel worse.

When your soul mate raises the subject of racism, be sure to listen with respect and sensitivity. The first step is to acknowledge the reality of the experience. Don't contradict someone else's interpretation of what happened and never be dismissive, even if you think a complaint is being blown out of proportion. There's nothing more unproductive than saying, "You're just being paranoid." A much better approach is to say, "You are obviously very upset. Let's look at what happened to see if you are viewing the situation objectively." By offering empathy and understanding, you can help diffuse any anger or shame your partner may be feeling and together identify productive ways to address the situation.

Here is a model of how soul mates can talk about the humiliation of a racist experience.

Jan comes home upset because she had been insulted at the gas station. Although she had been first in line, the attendant deliberately ignored her, politely filling up the tank of two other customers before turning to her with a scowl. As Jan tells her story, her husband, Benjamin, listens closely, occasionally repeating her words back to her. If you are unaccustomed to this technique, it may feel a bit awkward at first but it is an important way of letting the other party know you are listening and affirming his message.

"You were first and he served someone else who came in after you?"

Reassured by his interest, Jan volunteers more information. "Yes, he waited on some White guy in a fancy sports car."

"What else happened and how did you feel?" says Ben, which tells Jan he cares about her feelings. Ben has yet to offer an opinion or a judgment on the situation; at this point, he is collecting information so that he fully understands the situation.

Once all the facts are on the table, the air is cleared to discuss the next steps rationally. Ben may ask an open-ended question: "What would you like to do about it?"

That forces Jan to define her needs clearly. "I'd like you to confront that man, Ben."

Once he understands what Jan wants from him, Ben may agree to it or he may want to discuss the situation further, perhaps suggesting that they go directly to the manager or urging her to set the incident aside. Whatever happens next, the discussion itself minimizes the risk that an unpleasant experience outside the home will introduce tension between soul mates.

CROSSING THE COLOR LINE

In both African-American and White circles, there has been an acceptance of interracial dating in recent years that is greater than at any other time in American history. If both parties respect each other, honor their unique histories, and maintain a strong sense of themselves, we believe this development is a welcome sign of a greater appreciation for our common humanity.

However, Black men or women who date almost exclusively in White circles often have psychological issues they have not fully resolved. Problems of self-esteem or a discomfort with their own racial identity can lead men or women to devalue and reject others in their own community. For example, a woman may have internalized the myth that Caucasian features are more attractive than African ones and may not see the beauty in a man of color. A man may rebel against the seeds of self-hatred that were planted when his father said scornfully, "Black women are all you're going to get."

Sometimes, Black folks see White lovers as status symbols, signs they have reached the pinnacle of mainstream success. A woman's internal monologue might go, "Now that I've made it,

I'm going to get me the ultimate prize—a White boy." Sometimes, a power trip is involved—White women were for so long forbidden fruit that a Black man may now relish the prospect of a conquest. Or he may be consciously rejecting childhood messages that warned him never to cross the color line.

James came to us when he was seriously considering leaving his wife of fourteen years to pursue a relationship with one of his White colleagues. After learning that Darlene was scheduled to counsel him, he abruptly left our office and later telephoned to say that he had suddenly taken ill. Derek convinced him to return for therapy and during his first session, which we both attended, he admitted to fearing that a Black female therapist would disapprove of his sexual involvement with a White woman.

Actually, as therapists we never condemn the choices that our clients make and personally we have no problem with interracial relationships so long as they are pursued from a foundation of self-respect and do not involve a rejection of ethnic pride. Our role was not to tell James what to do but to help him understand his motivations and needs so that he could make healthy choices.

Although his coworker eventually broke off their relationship, she served as a catalyst for a level of internal scrutiny he had studiously avoided in the past. In therapy, James revealed that he had been raised in an abusive family; his father drank heavily and belittled his wife and children. He also taught James that White women were the ultimate prize, but one that would forever be beyond his reach. "You're never going to find anyone better than a Black bitch," the self-hating man would say. "That's all you deserve."

As an adult, James married a Black woman but never confronted the attitudes implanted in his youth. The contempt instilled by his father lingered, although he felt terribly guilty about it. By guiding James through the memories of his past, we helped him understand why he was so tantalized by White women and how his self-doubts prevented him from seeing Black women more positively.

Soul mates of different skin colors need to be especially sensitive to issues relating to racial identity and to encounters with discrimination. This is best fostered by creating an atmosphere in which it feels safe to talk.

In order to foster empathy in an interracial relationship, we sometimes suggest an outing based on an experience in Darlene's childhood. Years ago, she was on a ski trip with schoolmates, who were all White. On the slopes she spotted another Black girl about her age and they waved to each other. Within minutes Darlene skied over and they began chatting like old friends. Some of Darlene's classmates were astonished to learn the two girls had never met before and could not understand why they would seek each other out. "Oh Darlene, you're one of us," they told her. "We never make you feel left out." Darlene suggested to her closest White friend that she spend just a few hours in an all-Black environment to see how it felt. Her friend did just that and to this day still talks about how the experience heightened her sensitivity.

Sometimes a couple needs to be awakened to conflicts that are linked to ethnic differences. When Sue and Al sought therapy, for example, they scoffed at the suggestion of friends that they were troubled by issues of race. After a lot of soul-searching, however, Al began to admit his feelings of isolation in the White community where they lived and affirm his need for closer connections with Black peers.

His candor opened the way for a frank exploration of racial issues and Sue revealed that she felt like an outsider when Al's extended family assembled to celebrate the holidays. His sisters always addressed her with icy politeness and Sue was never quite sure whether they resented her marriage or just felt ill at ease in her presence. Despite their five-year marriage, Sue and Al had never confronted these long-festering issues because they did not want to admit that race could be a source of struggle between them. When they finally did, both of them were relieved to find that candid dialogue brought them even closer.

Family, Friends, and Spirituality

As if sex and infidelity, money and careers, and racial and gender identity weren't enough to trouble soul mates, conflicts about family bonds, friendship, and religion also pose complex challenges to intimacy. Whether you are single or deeply involved with a partner, the kinship and spiritual traditions with which you were raised and your attitudes toward them today will influence your search for a soul mate and how you relate once you meet someone special. These are some of the delicate questions you may have to consider: What do you do if your relatives have a long-standing Christmas tradition while your Afrocentric partner wants to make Kwanzaa the major year-end celebration? How do you respond to a judgmental relative who thinks your single life-style is self-indulgent or unseemly? How can you set limits that establish your autonomy and preserve your privacy without insulting beloved family members or shutting them out altogether? How will you feel when a weekend date gets canceled because your partner has to take an out-of-town business colleague of the opposite sex to dinner? What do you do if your partner says he loves you but insists that you convert to Catholicism before he will make a commitment?

Many of your most fundamental values are reflected in how you answer these questions. Finding ways to remain true to your beliefs, respectful of your kin, loyal to your friends, and responsive to the needs of a soul mate is not easy—but it can be done. Respect and open communication are the tools that will help you find common ground with a partner, even when family tradition and personal experience have given you very different outlooks.

Our Family Structure

The legacy of the extended family, which had its origins in Africa, is still thriving in the homes of many African-Americans. It is not unusual to meet Black folks who have been raised by grandparents, aunts and uncles, or other kin. Several generations of relatives may live in close proximity or get together often. Many of us count godparents or family friends we have known from childhood in the tight circle of our extended family. Through a network of kinship ties, we gain role models for our children, sources of emotional or financial support, and dependable allies in a sometimes scary and uncertain world. Supportive kin stand by our sides to celebrate good fortune when it occurs and to lend a hand when times are tough. Often, they may also be cherished confidants—perhaps you still consult with a favored aunt whenever you confront a difficult decision or schedule family forums on a regular basis to talk about pressing concerns.

If an extended family is central to your life, you are a part of something very special but you probably also experience its complications. Single people sometimes find that kin seek to impose their own norms and expectations, advise them about the suitability of every date, or urge them to try harder to find a partner and to settle down. "You know there aren't too many Black men around," Jo's cousin used to say. "Better get attached to someone who has a good job and will take care of you, even if you don't feel passionately about him." Although Jo was self-sufficient and proud of her independence, her cousin's message made her feel doubtful and guilty about how she chose to live her life.

If you are married or dating someone seriously, your soul mate will hopefully respect and appreciate the love of your extended family, but here too the joys may be tempered by pressure. Family members may pelt you both with unsolicited advice, criticize your household or child-rearing decisions, knock on your door without advance warning, or impose seemingly endless social obligations on you. "Naturally, you'll be coming to our house for Thanksgiving," a well-intentioned grandparent might say, failing to consider your own plans or the possibility that you have commitments to the other side of the family.

Margaret is a client of ours who has had to deal with boundary issues in order to establish some appropriate distance from her close-knit family. As a single, professional woman in her late twenties with younger sisters who were already married, Margaret was made to feel as though time were running out. "An older woman isn't of much interest to men," her relatives would say. "You aren't getting any younger." Margaret had made a promise to herself to be married by the age of thirty in order to please her family. When she began dating Stan, she pushed him hard for a commitment and entered therapy complaining that despite his sincere interest in her, he was fearful of getting married. In counseling we helped her distinguish between a genuine desire, which was to cultivate and deepen her relationship with Stan, and the artificial time frame she had imposed in response to family pressures.

A similar example of excessive family influence comes from the story of a couple who sought counseling support after deciding to end their marriage. After long, wrenching discussions, they had resolved the issue in their own minds and both agreed that divorce was the right decision. The problem that brought them into therapy was how to handle the opposition of their families. Again we emphasized their rights as autonomous adults entitled to control their own lives; certain decisions were theirs alone to make.

Even if your family relationships don't cause conflicts for you, they may spark resentment or jealousy from your partner. "I don't know what Joe gets out of our relationship," complained Marilyn. "When anything goes wrong, his mama or sister are always standing right by his side to comfort him. He sure doesn't need me to meet his emotional needs."

Herbert feels the same way about the woman with whom he lives. "She comes home from work, waves hello to me, and gets right on the phone so she can tell her godmother all about her day. I'm glad she's got such a strong family but I feel like I'm an outsider."

If you or your partner feel cut off from intimacy because family members are so often on the scene, it is important to talk about your issues and state your needs explicitly. Rather than lashing out—"Your sister's kids are always in my hair" or "You care more about providing companionship to your grandparents than about being there for me"—soul mates should verbalize their concerns with "I" statements. An example is: "I respect your commitment to take care of your sister's kids while she is at work but I feel overwhelmed and neglected at times. I think we are stretching ourselves too thin. How can we arrange our lives so that we can be alone together a little more often?" That clarifies your own emotional concerns while encouraging your partner to propose workable solutions.

Here are some other guidelines for dealing with your kin or the relatives of someone you are dating:

Understand the origins of your attitudes toward family. The way you feel about kinship ties today was shaped largely by what happened to you as a child. If you were raised in a functional extended family, instilled with a sense of worth, and inspired by the role models around you, early ties may retain their central place in your life. However, the nuclear family has historically been the norm in American society and many Black children who were raised in other environments, especially without the presence of a father, felt abnormal in their communities or at school. Unless relatives helped affirm the validity of your family structure, painful memories of being "different" may linger into adulthood. If you internalized negative messages from childhood, you may now try to distance yourself from your extended family or avoid romances with partners who have their own strong family ties.

The experience of being reared in a nuclear family has its own influence. It is likely that you will have a strong sense of privacy and may not be accustomed to involving relatives in the intimate details of your life. If you become involved with a partner from an extended family, you may have a lot of adjusting to do. At times you may even feel strangled by the demands of relatives. By tracing your discomfort to its roots in your own experiences, you can at least understand how your perspectives were formed and why family issues now create conflicts. It helps to remember that nuclear and extended families are both healthy environments so long as they affirm the value of each of their members.

Strive to accommodate each other. There is no doubt about it—family members sometimes place demands on you, disrupt your plans for an intimate weekend, or assume the right to offer unsolicited advice. You may have to endure well-intentioned but intrusive inquires about someone you are dating. At times you will prefer to be watching a football game when you are expected to attend a family gathering. In moments of need you may be asked to provide emotional, financial, or logistical support to your soul mate's kin, even if it is inconvenient or a hardship.

There will be instances when you must say no to family because you have other obligations or because someone's request is simply not reasonable. That's okay and you should not feel guilty about speaking plainly; healthy families respect the autonomy of their members. On the other hand, when it is possible to be accommodating, it is worthwhile to try. Compromises and modest sacrifices speak volumes about your respect for family; your understanding and patience will also win enormous gratitude from your soul mate.

Address real issues. Sometimes our partners say one thing about family but mean another. This is not because they are being deceitful but because they are somewhat out of touch with their own emotional responses. Soon after Sally's nephew came to live in their house, Austin began complaining about the young teenager. "I don't like that boy, Sally," said Austin. "He's causing problems for us." By mirroring his comments back to him—"I hear you saying that my nephew is causing difficulties for our relationship"—and then asking questions to elicit further details, Sally was able to uncover the true source of Austin's unhappiness. He finally admitted that he resented the energy that Sally invested in her nephew's adjustment and wondered when their lives would return to normal. Once he clarified his feelings, Sally was able to reassure Austin and to propose some specific ways for them to carve out more intimate time together.

Set boundaries. While interdependent family bonds provide a powerful sense of connectedness and can be wonderfully rewarding, intrusive relationships can make you feel that your personal space is being violated. No matter how much they love you, your relatives do not have the right to dictate your behavior. The deference rightfully given to elders in the family because of their position and status needs to be weighed against your legitimate needs. Whether you are single or paired off, you are an adult who is entitled to privacy and the right to make your own decisions.

To achieve a balance between personal autonomy and family

obligations, you must learn to draw boundaries and to let your relatives know when their good intentions and genuine concern have crossed the line into interference. This means asserting yourself firmly, yet tactfully, just as you have been learning to do in your love relationships.

It helps to affirm good intentions before asking a relative to cool it. "Mama, you know how much we appreciate your interest in Jack but the decision about which church our son will attend is in our hands. It is important to me that you respect my rights here." Remember that no one can live your life for you; insist that your family give you room to breathe and the right to make your own mistakes and to learn from them.

Speak up for your partner. It is important to support your soul mate if he or she clashes with family members. Celia, an administrator at a mostly White college, and Bob, who organized tenants in an all-Black housing project, were comfortable with their differing levels of ethnic identity, but Bob's family complained that Celia acted as if she were better than other Black folks. Celia resented their thinly disguised hostility and felt angry that Bob did not speak up for her more directly. The issue came to a head when they both heard Bob's sister mutter, "I don't know why my brother wants to be involved with a girl who's nearly White, anyhow."

At first Bob shrugged off the remark but Celia refused to ignore it. She expressed her pain clearly, forcing Bob to deal with the matter. "It really hurt when your sister insulted me and you didn't say a word. Her remark was inappropriate and I wanted you to tell her so."

In therapy, Bob admitted that he had been putting up with his sister's comments in order to keep peace within the family. As he began to understand how his silence enabled the continuing insults, he recognized the importance of asserting himself. We also encouraged Celia to talk directly to her sister-in-law about her feelings. Although Celia and Bob's sister seemed unlikely to become the closest of friends, the relationship became much warmer once the couple helped his family to see that Celia was committed to her African-American roots, even though her manner of dress and speech were not Afrocentric by their definition. Over time, they began to appreciate her for who she is, and not who they thought she should be.

A Word on Blended Families

These days, with so many people getting together with a partner in their thirties or forties, many African-Americans are creating blended families, which are formed when one or both adults bring children from previous marriages into new relationships. If you become seriously involved with someone who already has children, or if you have them yourself, a new series of emotional challenges will be introduced into your lives.

Children may feel hurt, lonely, or confused and typically need to be convinced that they are still valued. In order to test a parent's love, some children may vent anger or deliberately misbehave. Others go to the opposite extreme, trying not to make waves and stifling strong emotions for fear of being abandoned. Children may also feel that getting close to your new partner is disloyal to the other parent. Adults will likely have their own complex responses with which to contend. A parent may feel a sense of divided loyalty, torn between wanting to devote attention to an unhappy child and to commit fully to a new partner. The new partner may withdraw from any child-rearing responsibilities in order to keep peace, or, conversely, assert strict authority in order to establish new ground rules for the family.

To prevent insecurities and power struggles from interfering with a relationship, everyone's concerns must be addressed. A couple must reassure all their children that they are loved unconditionally while resisting any subtle or not-so-subtle efforts to force a wedge between them. Children need to hear this message repeatedly: "I have a new relationship now and I am committed to it. I love you and I will always be there for you but I am also devoted to my new partner. I will work to maintain and strengthen both of these valuable relationships." Any disagreements you and your partner have about discipline or the best ways to manage a child's behavior should be ironed out behind closed doors; in public, it is important not to be pitted against one another by children seeking greater permissiveness. Try not to allow child rearing to consume all of your emotional energy—soul mates manage to stay lovers, as well as parents and stepparents. If necessary, set up a schedule that includes specific times to be alone with your new partner.

Why Friendships Matter

Love relationships cannot fulfill all of our needs for companionship and communication and we should not insist that they try to do so. We think it is healthy for couples to spend some of their time apart. By cultivating independent friendships, two people can more readily maintain a degree of individuality, form some of their own opinions, and cultivate interests that a partner may not share. Outside friendships also provide a source of stimulating ideas, insights, and even friendly gossip that give you something new to share with your partner.

Many brothers and sisters find it difficult to assign friends an appropriate place in their lives. Instead, they seem to chose between two extremes. Some people become so emotionally involved with a soul mate that they cut off most other social connections. They treat friends as stopgap companions who fill up evenings when they don't have a date. They may shamelessly break previous engagements if a man comes on the scene. "Girl, I never see Paula anymore since she got serious about Ralph," said Robin, expressing her exasperation with a good friend who lost interest in female companionship once she began dating someone steadily. "She doesn't have time for anything or anybody else and isn't interested in what is going on in my life anymore. I feel as though I have lost a friend."

By contrast, other people maintain attachments with friends that are too close to be healthy. Friendships that consume an excessive amount of time or emotional energy trespass into the private lives of soul mates and send a signal that something has gone wrong. A man who spends most of his evenings and weekends with his buddies, maybe on the basketball court or at the bar, is usually expressing ambivalence about making a total commitment. Latching onto the company of male friends becomes a way to withdraw from intimacy or to declare aggressively: "I can do my own thing, no one dominates me." A woman who talks excessively to a close girlfriend may not know how to communicate effectively with her partner nor realize that he feels cut off from her emotional life.

Soul mates manage to keep satisfying and stimulating friendships alive without allowing them to become intrusive. In mature, mutually nourishing relationships, people treasure old friends without using them as psychological weapons in battles against their partners. Welcoming friends into the social circles you share with a soul mate is one effective way to ease jealousy. That doesn't mean you stop seeing old friends by yourself but it allows your partner to feel more comfortable with your external friendships.

One of the most sensitive issues couples face is how to handle opposite-sex friendships. Especially in the early days of a romance, your partner's close ties with someone of the opposite sex may fuel insecurity and cause you to question the sincerity of his interest in you.

If your partner has overly strong emotional ties with someone else, the threat to your love can become very real. On the other hand, many people have close friendships, dating back many years, with members of the opposite sex. With so many more women in the workplace now, professional and business connections may also throw men and women together for extended periods of time. Their interactions need not have sexual overtones and the assumption that they do can be very irritating to men and women who are genuinely committed to monogamy. "Where is the idea coming from that all brothers are going to cheat on you?" asked George at one of our discussion sessions. "When I go out to lunch with a female colleague, my woman jumps down my throat. She is convinced I've got some sort of an ulterior motive."

A client of ours named Ruth described a scene that has become familiar in her relationship. "Allan just about explodes every time Jefferson calls me," she said. "I've known that boy since we were both in diapers but my man's got it in his head that there is something else between us. He just won't accept me having a close male friend."

Because Allan reacts angrily to Jefferson's phone calls, Ruth becomes hostile. "Your jealousy is just crazy and I don't want to hear about it anymore," she sometimes yells at him. "I'll talk to Jefferson anytime I want to and there's nothing you can do about it."

Instead of approaching the "Jefferson problem" in a way that almost guarantees tension will escalate, Ruth and Allan should apply the techniques of assertive communication to resolve the issue.

The first step is for Allan to set aside his rage and to express his feelings clearly. He can say: "I feel uncomfortable with how close you seem to be to Jefferson. Can you help me understand your friendship with him?"

Ruth then validates Allan's concern, rather than accusing him of jealousy, by saying: "I understand that you have some nagging questions." Next, she offers a clarification to help Allan feel more secure. "Jefferson is an old family friend whose advice has always meant a lot to me."

Notice that Ruth does not concede her rights to maintain an important friendship. Instead, she signals her willingness to listen to Allan's concerns and to alleviate his doubts. That encourages Allan to elaborate on the cause of his insecurity and to propose solutions that accommodate both of their needs.

Every couple needs to set their own limits but a good general policy about friendships—whether they are with women or men—is this: Give each other some breathing room and insist on some for yourself. Ask for space and be willing to grant it to your soul mate. Remember: Commitment does not mean bondage. In a healthy soul-mate relationship, neither party should have to sacrifice valued friendships. Two people who love each other must also learn to trust each other.

At the same time, both parties need to understand that friendships often have sexual overtones. If they are there, admit your feelings of attraction, then set appropriate limits and stick to them. If one party continually violates agreed-upon relationship boundaries, a platonic friendship probably won't work.

Spirituality and Religion

The Black church has historically played an important role in our spiritual, community, and family lives. According to a recent Gallop poll, African-Americans are the "most religious" ethnic group in the United States. Our people embrace many faiths. We are Baptists, Methodists, and Catholics, Presbyterians and Episcopalians, Muslims and Pentecostals. There are also Seventh-Day Adventists, Jehovah's Witnesses, Hindus, Buddhists, and Jews within our ranks. Some Black folks have remained with the faith in which they were raised, others have converted to different religions as adults.

The range of our religious beliefs and practices is almost infinite. Some people interpret the Bible literally, others view its messages only as parables intended to provide guidance. Some churches encourage congregants to "get the Spirit" and declare themselves reborn while others are more reserved in their expressions of faith. Even African-Americans who have drifted away from organized religion may still return when they face tough times or difficult decisions. And those who do not, often pursue spiritual inspiration and uplift through private meditation, personal quests for inner knowledge, and Afrocentric cultural experiences.

Whatever your spiritual beliefs, they are likely to be the foundation upon which you base many of your decisions about education, sexuality, use of leisure time, child rearing, and even diet. For that reason, differing religious traditions can cause rifts between soul mates that are not easy to reconcile. However, faith can also be a tool of reconciliation and a source of sustenance and inspiration. Many couples turn to religion to find the strength, courage, and confidence they need to repair troubled relationships. For example, we know a deeply religious couple who were on the verge of splitting up when they turned to their minister for guidance. The minister acknowledged that the church allowed divorce but reminded them: "In our faith, we believe men and women are brought together by God. That means you should not give up easily, even when all the differences between you seem impossible to reconcile. You should first work toward saving your marriage."

Instead of bailing out, this couple took the minister's message to heart. Their religious faith and worship practices provided the spiritual strength to pursue treatment and they entered therapy, committed to the hard work of confronting their conflicts. We have watched with excitement as they make great strides in resolving fundamental differences.

Typically, religious conflicts arise when two people can't—or won't—find ways to compromise in their approach to worship. One woman felt that her man's refusal to attend her church sent

a message that said, "My religion is more important than yours."
A man we counseled ended a relationship because he felt insulted
by his lady's indifference to his religious beliefs. Another man
tried to deemphasize his faith after becoming involved with a
woman who rejected organized religion, and then had to deal
with the feelings of loss and resentment that arose once he stopped
attending church.

When one partner is dogmatic, critical, or inclined toward a
holier-than-thou attitude, it is especially hard to establish a climate for negotiation. Mary kept saying to Pat, the man she was
dating, "You have not been saved. I have made my commitment
to Christ while you remain of the world." Her judgmental dec-
laration left him little room to establish the legitimacy of his own
beliefs.

Quan and Dee's story illustrates the need to approach religion
in a respectful way and to stay alert to each other's sensitivities.
When Quan invited Dee to attend his church, she was delighted
because a belief in God and the inspirational power of spirituality
had always been important to her. Nothing in her own conservative Protestant background, however, had prepared her for
Quan's congregation. The preacher spoke passionately about sin
and salvation and as the service progressed, the room seemed to
catch fire. Members of the congregation shouted loud "amens"
from time to time and everyone in the room swayed back and
forth, their arms raised high in the air. Quan seemed right at
home but Dee was overwhelmed, having learned in childhood
to control her emotions and express religious feelings privately.

Couples like Quan and Dee need to be flexible, respectful,
and accommodating in order to sustain a relationship. Although
soul mates do not have to belong to the same church or pursue
exactly the same spiritual path, they need to be aware of their
differences and find ways to deal with them. To defuse the hot
buttons of religion and faith, it helps to undertake a little self-
analysis. Here are some questions to think about:

What kind of religious beliefs do you have?

How important is your faith?

How do you express your religious beliefs?

Do you feel comfortable with your partner's religion?

Next, you should ask the same questions about your partner's life. The answers will alert you to potential conflicts.

Finally, you need to identify the possibilities for compromise. Some couples are content to attend services separately, others rotate between two places of worship. An alternative is to attend each other's church social events, such as picnics and dances, while continuing to worship independently. Some people are willing to convert to another faith, either because religion did not play a powerful role in their own upbringing or because they are content to express spirituality through more than one system of organized worship. To identify the ways that work for *you*, ask yourself the following questions:

Are you comfortable attending church alone?

Are you willing to attend services at your partner's church from time to time?

Is your partner willing to attend services at your church from time to time?

Is it important to your partner that you convert to his or her faith?

Would you consider converting to another faith?

Whatever solutions you negotiate should allow both partners to remain true to themselves. One person may say, "I respect your religious beliefs but I also value a connection with my church. It is important to me to hear my own minister every Sunday. Are there other ways that we can express our commitment to God together?" Notice that she first validates her partner's needs, then expresses her own, and concludes with an open-ended question that affirms her willingness to find common ground.

The interpersonal and spiritual issues we have been addressing in this chapter pose some especially tough challenges because they strike at the heart of who we are as people. Strong, affirming family ties, close friendships, and sustaining faith can enrich our lives in wonderful ways and draw soul mates close together. But when family or friendship ties become intrusive, or when religious divisions cause pain, they can sever a promising relationship. If you understand how your partner's attitudes have been shaped by upbringing and personal experience, if you respect your differences, and if you are willing to work to bridge the gap that divides you, you may be able to clear a path toward victory.

Empowering
the Black
Community

▲ ▼

Friends, Lovers, and Soul Mates has tried to guide you on a journey of self-discovery and change. The first stage of healing the divisions between Black men and women involves doing some hard work on yourself. By confronting your past, you begin to understand the damage inflicted by negative role models, painful childhood experiences, and racism. Once you recognize how this has battered your self-esteem, you can begin working to erase destructive messages that keep you from loving yourself. Only when you have internalized the belief that you are worthy of respect will you have the confidence to accept a soul mate's love and to return it without reservation.

We also explored techniques for breaking down the barriers between brothers and sisters. Skills-building exercises were intended to help you improve your ability to communicate, negotiate, and compromise in order to confront conflict more effectively. This book also emphasized the importance of commitment and trust, provided guidelines for managing anger, and demonstrated the importance of treating each other fairly and with care. We also talked about the sensitive subjects of skin tone, money, jobs, sex, infidelity, family, and religion, and the ways each can help foster, rather than interfere with, love.

The immediate goal of all of these discussions is, of course, to help you break destructive patterns and relate to each other in new ways. But we hope this book can serve a broader purpose as well. In the Afrocentric world view, we live not only for ourselves, but for others. Soul mates who find ways to breathe life into a philosophy of love, commitment, caring, and trust create the building blocks of strong communities.

We believe that many of the issues that divide Black men and women in their personal relationships also weaken us collectively. Self-doubt and self-loathing have as large a role in the troubles facing the African-American community—from poverty and substance abuse to teenage pregnancy and crime—as they do in blocking intimacy between men and women. Fortunately, the same tools that help us resolve personal conflicts and cement soul-mate bonds can be used to strengthen and empower our community. Determination, hope, unity, and a belief that change is possible are all fundamental, as are the Afrocentric principles of sacrifice, inspiration, vision, and victory. We also believe that a connection with a source of spirituality gives soul mates inner strength as they strive to find meaning in their lives and relationships.

One message of this book has been that it is possible to overcome the past, break destructive patterns, and learn to relate to other adults in positive, self-affirming ways. However, it is not easy and the next generation of Black children deserve a different legacy. If we can teach them from infancy to love themselves, they will be greatly advantaged when they are beginning to learn how to love others. If we can model affirmative, loving relationships for them, they will be that much better prepared to become soul mates themselves.

As we develop pride in ourselves, both as individuals and as couples, we begin to validate and affirm ourselves as a culture.

Soul mates who work together to build a better world speak with a single voice about the possibility of making constructive changes. At times, they may be focused inward, enjoying the comforts of home or the extraordinary experience of raising children. But they recognize that time devoted to community activities is also time that greatly enriches their lives as a couple.

In our own lives, a dedication to uplifting others and a shared sense of mission has helped bring us close together. Before we met, we each had relationships with other people but never felt satisfied. Those connections always seemed to be focused on the "here and now," and the companionship was nice but we felt that something was always missing. When we met at a convention of the American Psychological Association, we knew right away that we shared something bigger than ourselves. In an environment where so many of our colleagues were discussing their latest publications and the hottest new research, the two of us quickly began talking about our families and our shared goals of enriching the lives of our own people. In the years of dating, marriage, and child rearing that have followed, we have both remained deeply committed to returning something to the African-American community that has given us so much.

By reaching out to our brothers and sisters and sharing in the life of the community through volunteer work, Black-focused cultural events, and political forums, soul mates can transcend the negative forces encountered in our daily existence. Black men and women who love each other and work in unity toward common goals empower themselves, and, in doing so, empower all African-Americans. Couples who share a vision and know the importance of nurturing each other, who manage conflicts through cooperation and compromise, and who cultivate common ground are models for their peers. They are also a beacon of hope for the Black men and women now coming of age and looking for their own soul mates.

THE ART OF BECOMING SOULMATES

1. Becoming soul mates is an active process that requires commitment to the principles of vision, victory, sacrifice, inspiration, and balance. It is a cognitive and emotional pledge of support.
2. Becoming soul mates requires spiritual and emotional intimacy and the creation of a haven in which both partners feel safe from criticism and need not be defensive.
3. Becoming soul mates means understanding that we all have childhood baggage that has to be unpacked.
4. Becoming soul mates means eliminating the barriers to intimacy and putting each other first.
5. Becoming soul mates means making time for fun, romance, solitude, play, surprises, and passion.
6. Becoming soul mates means being supportive, complimenting each other, and communicating openly, honestly, and assertively.

7. Becoming soul mates means loving, touching, pleasing, and soothing.
8. Becoming soul mates means being reliable, dependable, and loyal.

For information and referrals about professional counseling, including sources of culturally sensitive therapy, contact any of the following groups:

The National Association of Black Social Workers
15231 W. McNicholas Avenue
Detroit, MI 48235
313-836-0210

Black Psychiatrists of America
2730 Adeline Street
Oakland, CA 94607
510-465-1800

Association of Black Psychologists
Box 55999
Washington, DC 20040
202-722-0808

INTRODUCTION

1. J. S. Mbiti, *African Religions and Philosophies*. Garden City, N.Y.: Anchor Books, 1969, p. 108.
2. Joseph L. White and Thomas A. Parham, *The Psychology of Blacks: An African-American Perspective*. Englewood Cliffs, N.J.: Prentice Hall, 1990.

CHAPTER ONE

1. Haki R. Madhubuti, *Black Men: Obsolete, Single, Dangerous? The Afrikan American Family in Transition: Essays in Discovery, Solution, and Hope*. Chicago: Third World Press, 1990, p. 16–17.
2. Ibid.

CHAPTER TWO

1. Na'im Akbar, *Chains and Images of Psychological Slavery*. Jersey City, N.J.: New Mind Productions, repr. of 1984 ed.
2. Molefi Kete Asante, *Afrocentricity: The Theory of Social Change*. 2d ed. Trenton, N.J.: Africa World Press, 1990.
3. Joseph L. White and Thomas A. Parham, *The Psychology of Blacks: An African-American Perspective*. Englewood Cliffs, N.J.: Prentice Hall, 1990.
4. Molefi Kete Asante, "Black Male and Female Relationships: An Afro-

centric Context," in *Black Men*, ed. Lawrence E. Gary. Beverly Hills: Sage Publications, 1981.

CHAPTER THREE

1. Nancy Boyd-Franklin, Ph.D., *Black Families in Therapy: A Multisystems Approach*. New York: Guilford Press, 1989, p. 235.
2. Bell Hooks and Cornel West, *Breaking Bread: Insurgent Black Intellectual Life*. Boston: South End Press, 1991, p. 107.

CHAPTER FOUR

1. Martin Luther King, *Where Do We Go from Here? Chaos or Community*. New York: Harper & Row, 1967, p. 107.

CHAPTER SIX

1. Nancy Boyd-Franklin, Ph.D., *Black Families in Therapy: A Multisystems Approach*. New York: Guilford Press, 1989, p. 235
2. Robert Alberti, *Your Perfect Right: A Guide to Assertive Living*. 6th ed. San Luis Obispo, Cal.: Impact Publications, Inc., 1990.

CHAPTER EIGHT

1. Haki R. Madhubuti, *Black Men: Obsolete, Single, Dangerous? The Afrikan American Family in Transition: Essays in Discovery, Solution, and Hope*. Chicago: Third World Press, 1990, p. 12.

I N D E X

abstinence, 159
abuse:
   in childhood, 18, 30, 62, 66, 67,
      93, 94, 95, 105, 110, 154–55,
      198
   as communication failure, 95
   in relationships, 79–80, 93–96,
      119
   verbal, 23, 80, 88
affairs, *see* infidelity
Africa, 33–37
   African-American heritage and,
      11, 33–37, 72–73, 74, 186–87,
      191
   Afrocentricity and, 49, 55
   kinship and community ties in,
      11, 35–36, 38, 41, 49–50, 202
   marriage in, 35, 36, 168
   monogamy and polygamy in, 36,
      168
   slave trade in, 33, 34–35, 38, 39
African-Americans:
   African and American identities
      balanced by, 50, 73

African heritage of, 11, 33–37,
   72–73, 74, 186–87, 191
American experiences of, 37–46,
   186, 192
collective identity of, 31–32, 35,
   50, 51, 218
dual existence of, 186–87
extended family tradition of, 37,
   56, 202–3, 205
in middle class, 44
as most religious U.S. ethnic
   group, 212
racial identity of, *see* racial identity
sense of identity in, 55–56; *see
   also* Afrocentricity
skin color of, 190–95
therapy and unique psychological
   needs of, 120–22
in underclass, 44
Whites' experiences vs. experiences of, 38, 44–45, 172, 180
African Religions and Philosophies
   (Mbiti), 11

exercise for identification of, 129–
131
passive communication:
defined, 125, 126
examples of, 128–29
exercise for identification of, 129–
131
postpartum depression, 192
"pretty boys," 84, 85
Psychology of Blacks, The (White
and Parham), 12, 50
put-downs, 23, 80, 88

racial identity:
duality of, 186–87
exercise for, 193–95
family's conflict with, 207
formation of, 72–75
internalized mainstream standards
and, 191–95, 197
interracial relationships and, 199–
200
negotiating differences in, 185–89
self-esteem and, 72–75, 190–95
skin color and, 190–95
as soul-mate characteristic, 22,
25–26
understanding myths of, 55–56
racism:
A-B-C theory and, 47
and accommodation of duality,
188
and balance of identity, 73
continuing pervasiveness of, 44,
57
Eurocentric world view and, 50
internalizing of, 46–47, 191–95
learned helplessness and, 113–14
myths vs. empowering beliefs
about, 57
as perceived threat to manhood,
23, 43, 48–49
relationships affected by, 11, 12,
14, 30, 53, 55, 81, 86, 93,
111–12, 180

sexism compared with, 76–77
talking about, 195–97
rational-emotive therapy, 47
relationships:
abuse in, 79–80, 93–96, 119
breaking old habits in, 89–93
clarifying goals in, 91–93
common mistakes in, 83–89
community empowered by, 14,
53–54, 217–19
games and hidden agendas in,
22–23, 24
healing wounds in, 13, 17
identifying destructive patterns in,
81–83
interracial, 197–200
patterns of, 79–99
possibility of change in, 117–18
racism's effect on, 11, 12, 14, 30,
53, 55, 81, 86, 93, 111–12,
180
role models for, 18, 66–68, 80–
81, 93, 123–24, 165
search for, 96–99
sex in balance of, 112, 119, 158–
159
warning signals in, 118–20
see also soul mates
religion, 212–16
conflicts on, 213–16
conversion and, 201–2, 212, 215
sexuality and, 154
see also spirituality
role models, 18, 66–68, 80–81, 93,
123–24, 165, 205

sacrifice, Afrocentric principle of,
51–52, 88, 89, 218
self-assessment exercises, *see* exercises, self-assessment
self-esteem, 61–78
of abused women, 94, 96
body image and, 65, 154
consumer culture and, 178
exercises for, 63–65, 91–93
as foundation for intimacy, 29

INDEX ▼ 237

information and referrals on, 222
rational-emotive, 47
supportive, 45–46
and unique psychological needs of
African-Americans, 120–22
trust:
exercise for, 108–10
infidelity and, 162–63, 165
intimacy and, 107–10, 118
as learned in childhood, 107–8
men's desire for, 23
Truth, Sojourner, 75–76

verbal abuse, 23, 80, 88
victory, Afrocentric principle of, 54–
55, 218
vision, Afrocentric principle of, 53–
54, 218
visualization, 64–65, 92, 107

Waiting to Exhale (McMillan), 13
West, Cornel, 77
White, Joseph L., 12, 50, 108
Whites:
African-American men as viewed
by, 20, 23
African-Americans' experiences
vs. experiences of, 38, 44–45,
172, 180
Afrocentricity and, 49, 73
alleged physiological superiority
of, 38
Eurocentric beliefs of, 50, 187
interracial relationships with,
197–200
racial identity and, 187–89, 193
sexism fostered by cultural mores
of, 183
"switching up" language and, 73–
74, 131
women, African-American:
abuse of, 93–96
admitting need for compassion to,
21
as "bitches," 114–15
commitment as viewed by, 106

control and, 26, 58, 86–87, 95–
96, 106, 114, 181
ease in sexuality of, 21–22
ethnic pride of, 22
families headed by, 45, 75, 90,
93–94, 115, 171, 177, 205
games played by, 23
greater financial resources of,
175–77
with hidden agenda, 22–23
honesty sought by, 24
men as viewed by, 11–12, 37,
115–16
men belittled by, 23, 80, 88
men's burdens assumed by, 80–
81, 87–88
men's views of, 11–12, 37, 114–
115
as "Miss Fix-it-alls," 80–81
most common mistakes made by,
86–89
myths vs. empowering beliefs
about sexuality of, 57
openly expressed affection sought
by, 24–25
put-downs by, 23, 80, 88
respect sought by, 26
sexism and, 75–78, 183
sexual needs of, 27, 152–53
sexual problems of, 152–53
and shortage of eligible men, 45,
46, 84–85, 164
slavery's legacy and, 40, 57
soul-mate characteristics sought
by, 24–27
soul-mate characteristics sought
in, 20–23
spiritual roots of, 22
as status seekers, 89, 90, 91, 170
stereotypes of, 114–15
strong, 22, 87
traditional expectations of, 173,
182–84
trust sought in, 23
work, household, sharing of, 133–
134, 173, 182–84